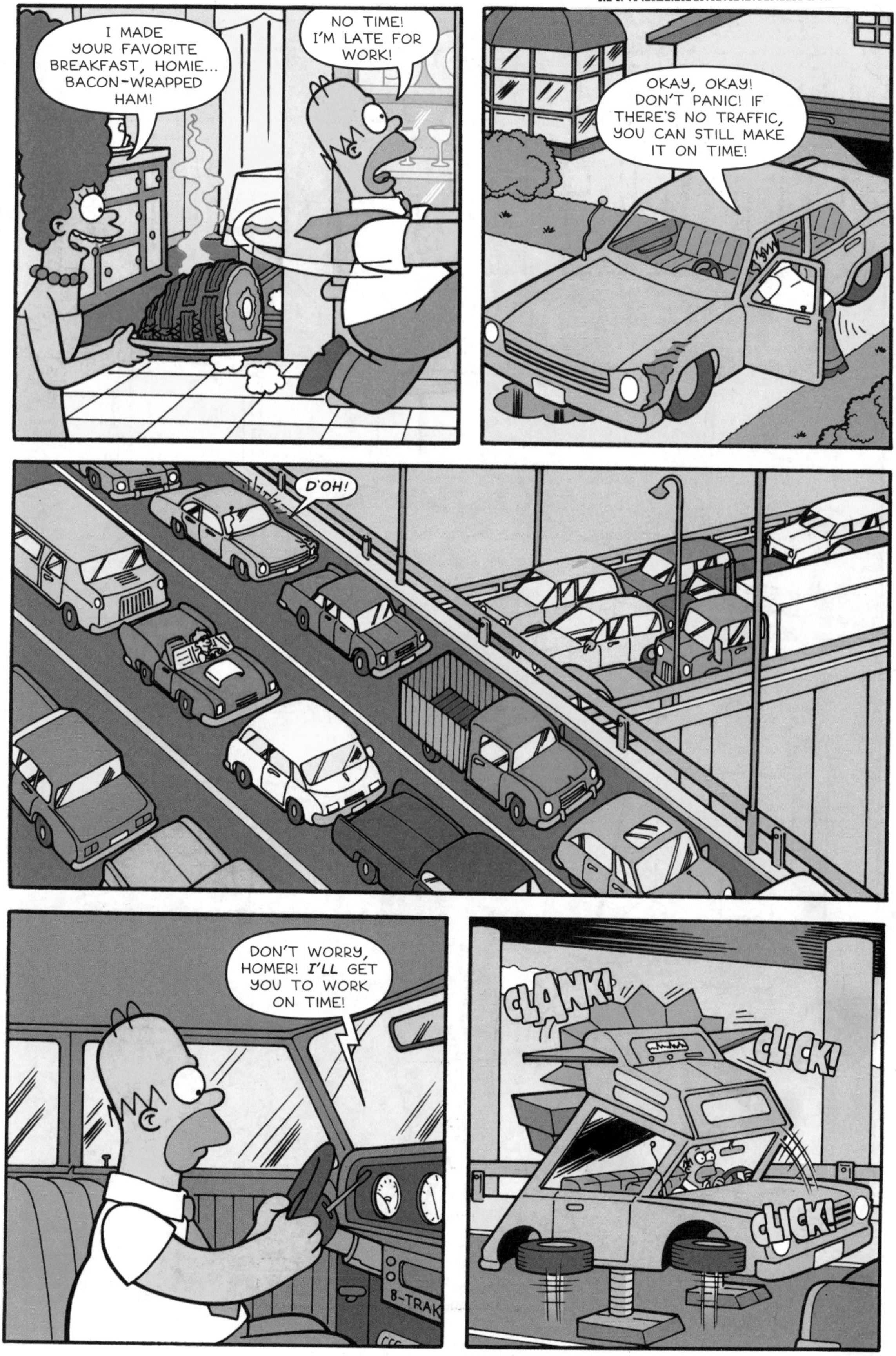

I MADE YOUR FAVORITE BREAKFAST, HOMIE... BACON-WRAPPED HAM!
NO TIME! I'M LATE FOR WORK!
OKAY, OKAY! DON'T PANIC! IF THERE'S NO TRAFFIC, YOU CAN STILL MAKE IT ON TIME!
D'OH!
DON'T WORRY, HOMER! *I'LL* GET YOU TO WORK ON TIME!
8-TRAK
CLANK!
CLICK!
CLICK!

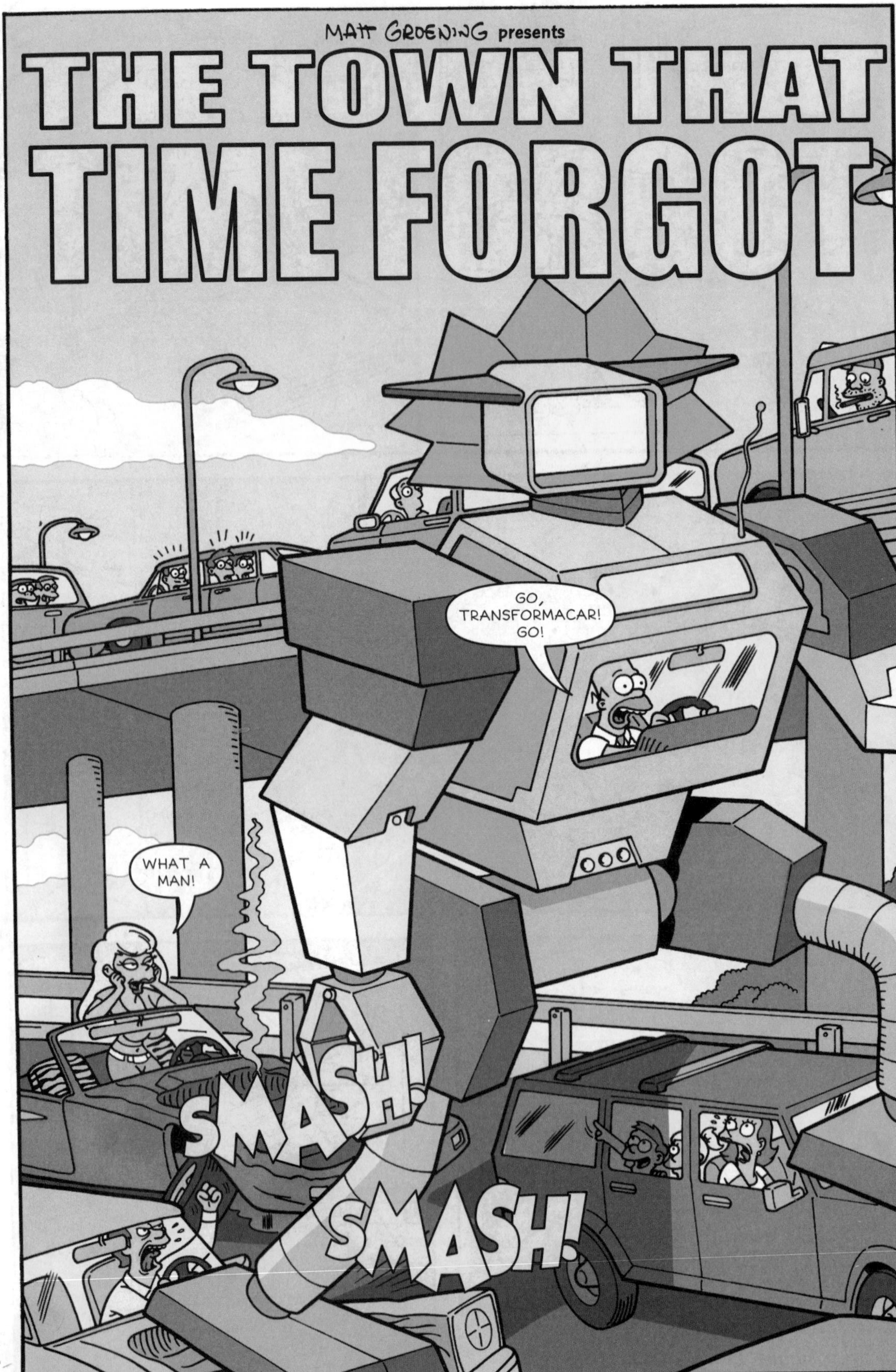
MATT GROENING presents
THE TOWN THAT TIME FORGOT
GO, TRANSFORMACAR! GO!
WHAT A MAN!
SMASH!
SMASH!

IAN BOOTHBY SCRIPT · PHIL ORTIZ PENCILS · MIKE DECARLO INKS · ART VILLANUEVA COLORS · KAREN BATES LETTERS · BILL MORRISON EDITOR

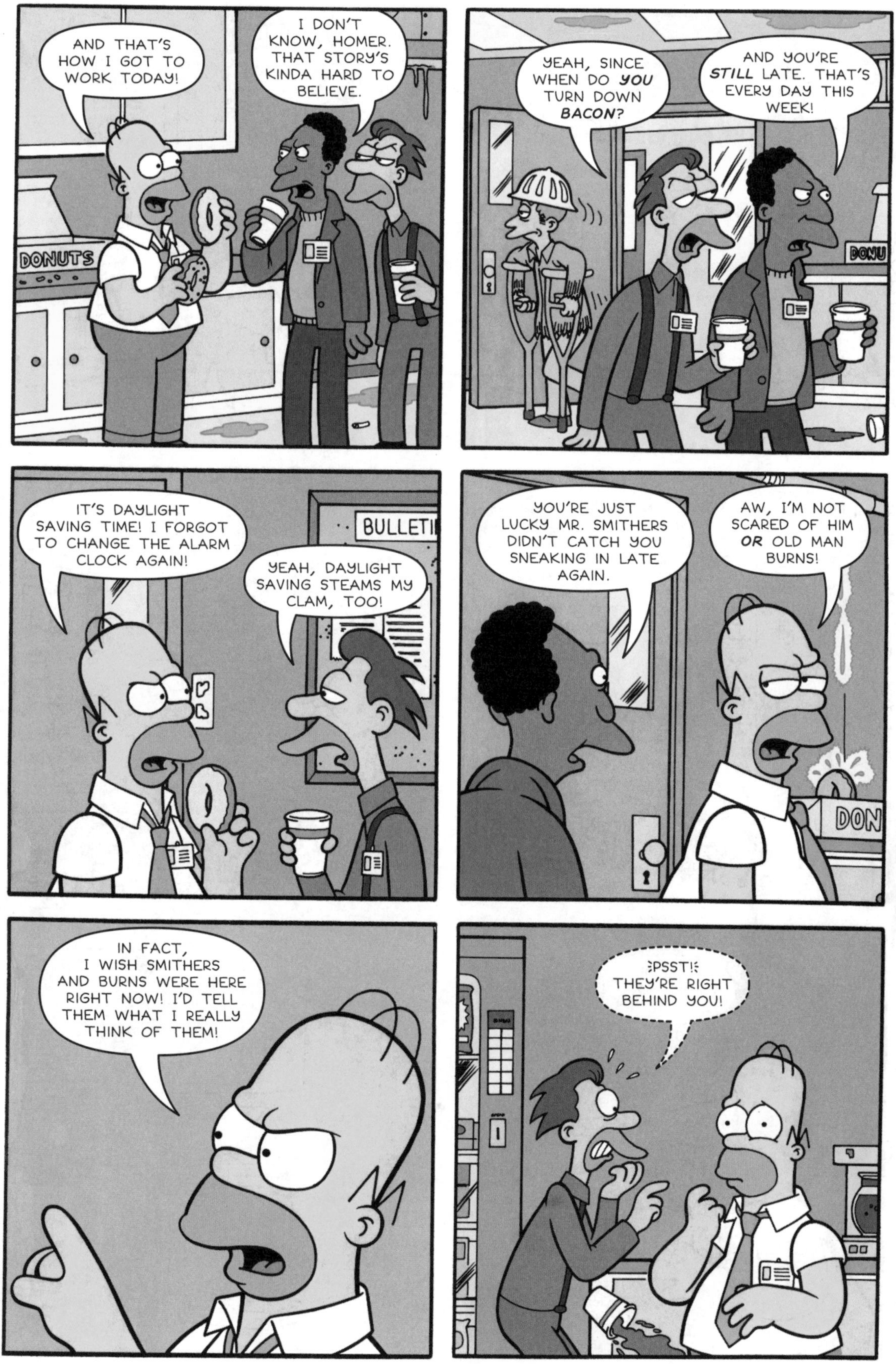
AND THAT'S HOW I GOT TO WORK TODAY!
I DON'T KNOW, HOMER. THAT STORY'S KINDA HARD TO BELIEVE.
DONUTS
YEAH, SINCE WHEN DO **YOU** TURN DOWN **BACON**?
AND YOU'RE **STILL** LATE. THAT'S EVERY DAY THIS WEEK!
IT'S DAYLIGHT SAVING TIME! I FORGOT TO CHANGE THE ALARM CLOCK AGAIN!
YEAH, DAYLIGHT SAVING STEAMS MY CLAM, TOO!
BULLETI
YOU'RE JUST LUCKY MR. SMITHERS DIDN'T CATCH YOU SNEAKING IN LATE AGAIN.
AW, I'M NOT SCARED OF HIM **OR** OLD MAN BURNS!
IN FACT, I WISH SMITHERS AND BURNS WERE HERE RIGHT NOW! I'D TELL THEM WHAT I REALLY THINK OF THEM!
PSST! THEY'RE RIGHT BEHIND YOU!

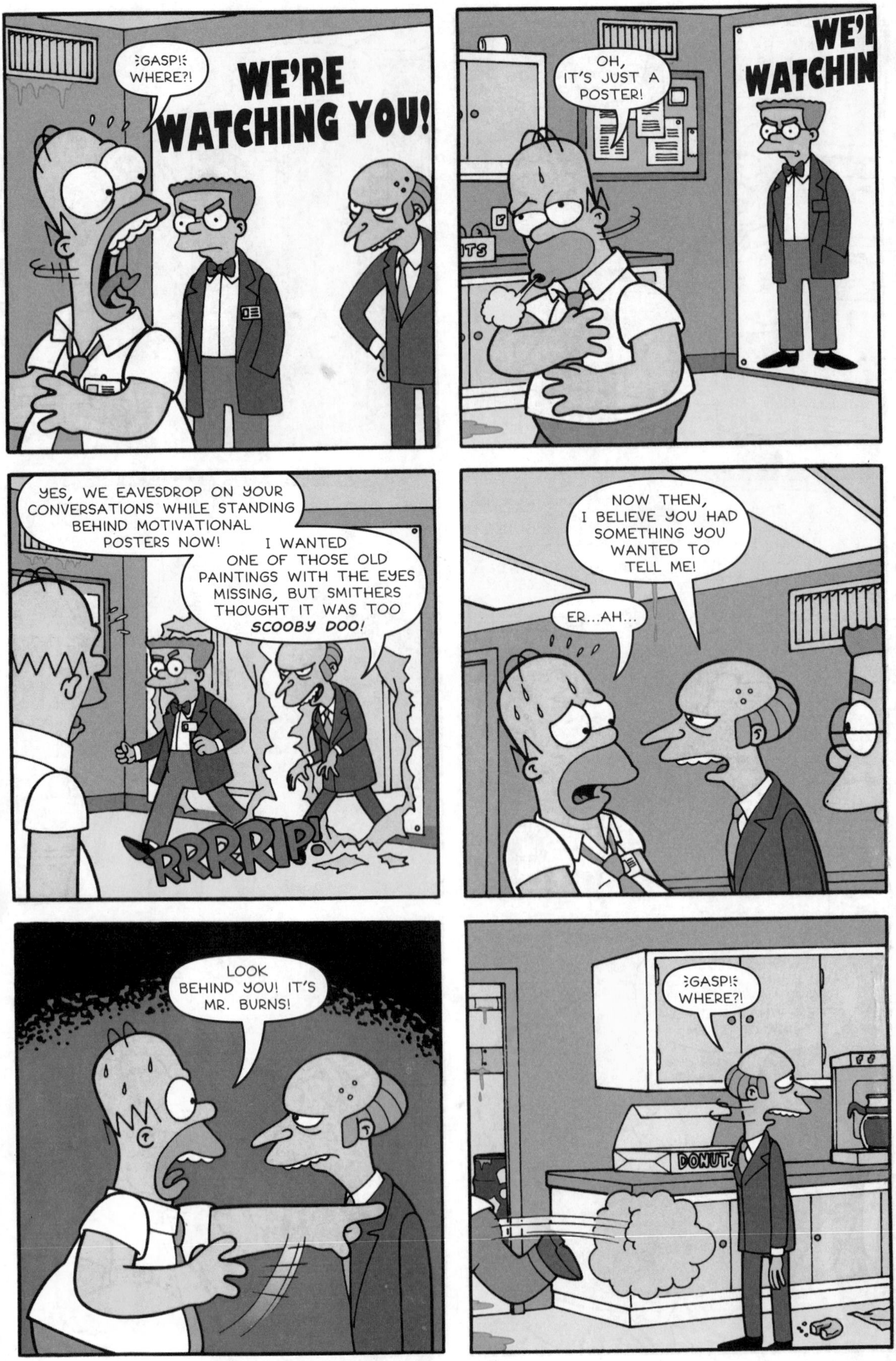

ᐅGASP!ᐊ WHERE?!
WE'RE WATCHING YOU!
OH, IT'S JUST A POSTER!
WE'
WATCHIN
YES, WE EAVESDROP ON YOUR CONVERSATIONS WHILE STANDING BEHIND MOTIVATIONAL POSTERS NOW!
I WANTED ONE OF THOSE OLD PAINTINGS WITH THE EYES MISSING, BUT SMITHERS THOUGHT IT WAS TOO *SCOOBY DOO*!
RRRRIP!
NOW THEN, I BELIEVE YOU HAD SOMETHING YOU WANTED TO TELL ME!
ER...AH...
LOOK BEHIND YOU! IT'S MR. BURNS!
ᐅGASP!ᐊ WHERE?!
DONUT

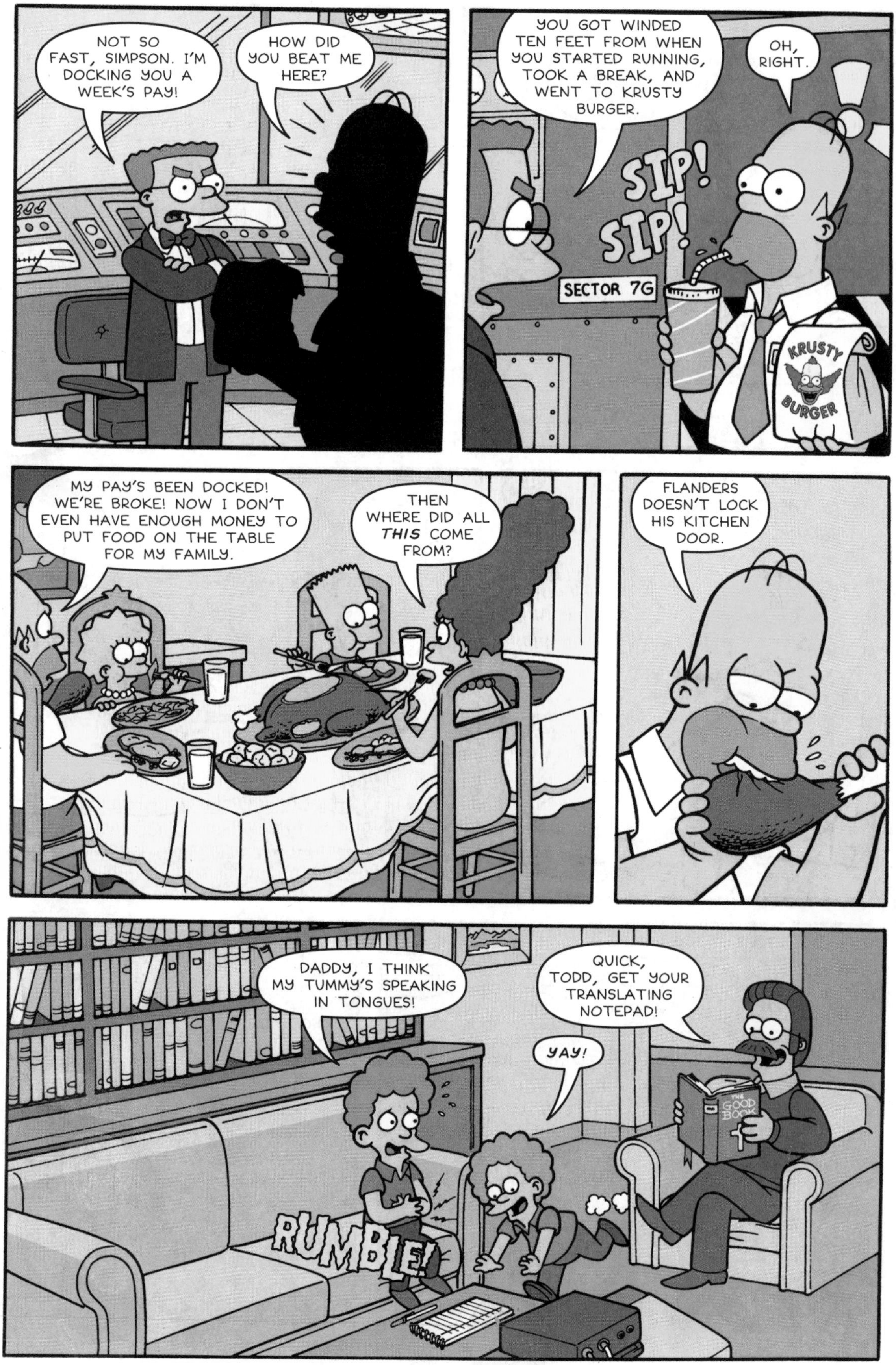
NOT SO FAST, SIMPSON. I'M DOCKING YOU A WEEK'S PAY!
HOW DID YOU BEAT ME HERE?
YOU GOT WINDED TEN FEET FROM WHEN YOU STARTED RUNNING, TOOK A BREAK, AND WENT TO KRUSTY BURGER.
OH, RIGHT.
SIP! SIP!
SECTOR 7G
KRUSTY BURGER
MY PAY'S BEEN DOCKED! WE'RE BROKE! NOW I DON'T EVEN HAVE ENOUGH MONEY TO PUT FOOD ON THE TABLE FOR MY FAMILY.
THEN WHERE DID ALL THIS COME FROM?
FLANDERS DOESN'T LOCK HIS KITCHEN DOOR.
DADDY, I THINK MY TUMMY'S SPEAKING IN TONGUES!
QUICK, TODD, GET YOUR TRANSLATING NOTEPAD!
YAY!
THE GOOD BOOK
RUMBLE!

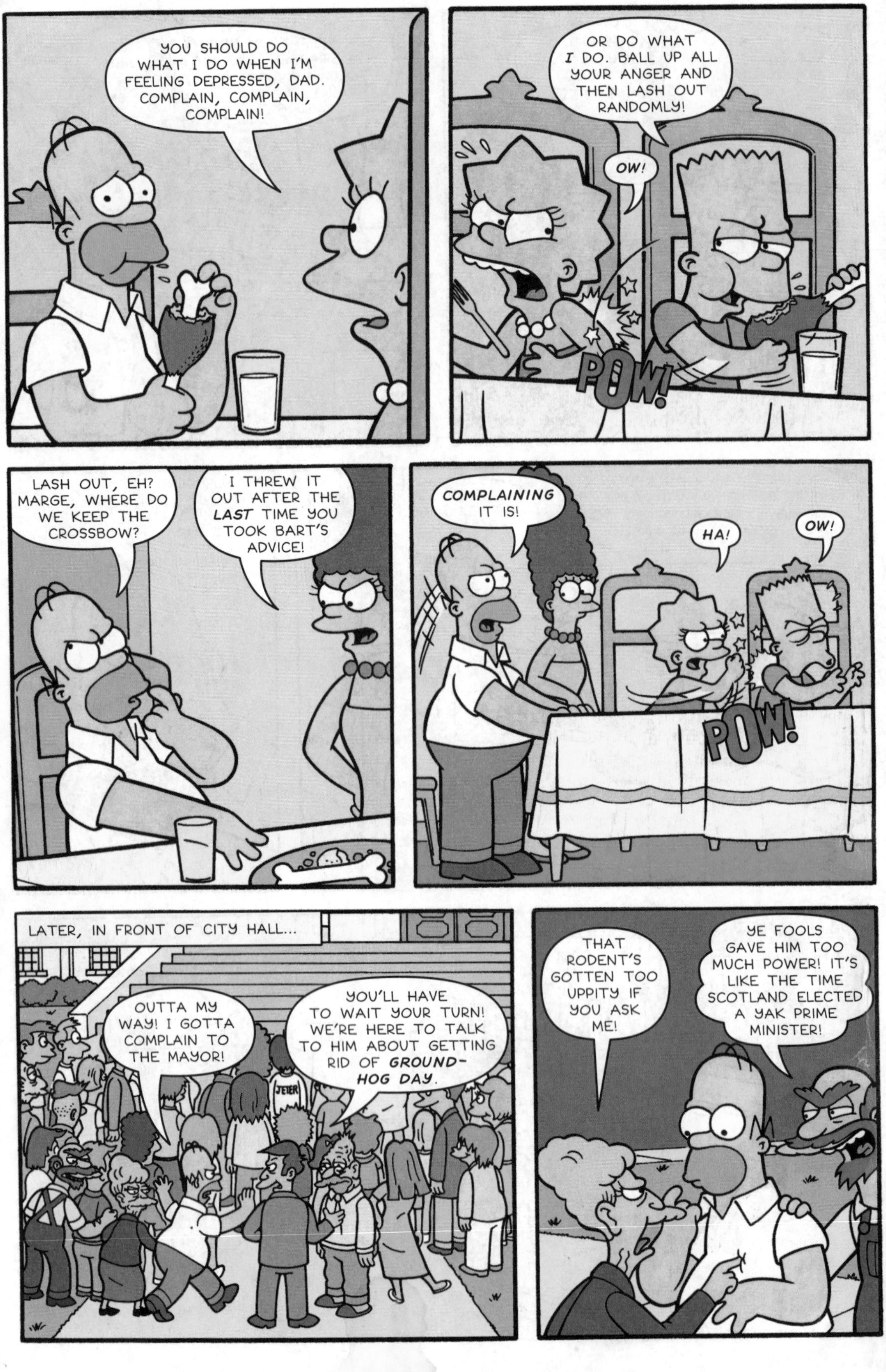
YOU SHOULD DO WHAT I DO WHEN I'M FEELING DEPRESSED, DAD. COMPLAIN, COMPLAIN, COMPLAIN!
OR DO WHAT *I* DO. BALL UP ALL YOUR ANGER AND THEN LASH OUT RANDOMLY!
OW!
POW!
LASH OUT, EH? MARGE, WHERE DO WE KEEP THE CROSSBOW?
I THREW IT OUT AFTER THE *LAST* TIME YOU TOOK BART'S ADVICE!
COMPLAINING IT IS!
HA!
OW!
POW!
LATER, IN FRONT OF CITY HALL...
OUTTA MY WAY! I GOTTA COMPLAIN TO THE MAYOR!
YOU'LL HAVE TO WAIT YOUR TURN! WE'RE HERE TO TALK TO HIM ABOUT GETTING RID OF *GROUND-HOG DAY*.
JETER
THAT RODENT'S GOTTEN TOO UPPITY IF YOU ASK ME!
YE FOOLS GAVE HIM TOO MUCH POWER! IT'S LIKE THE TIME SCOTLAND ELECTED A YAK PRIME MINISTER!

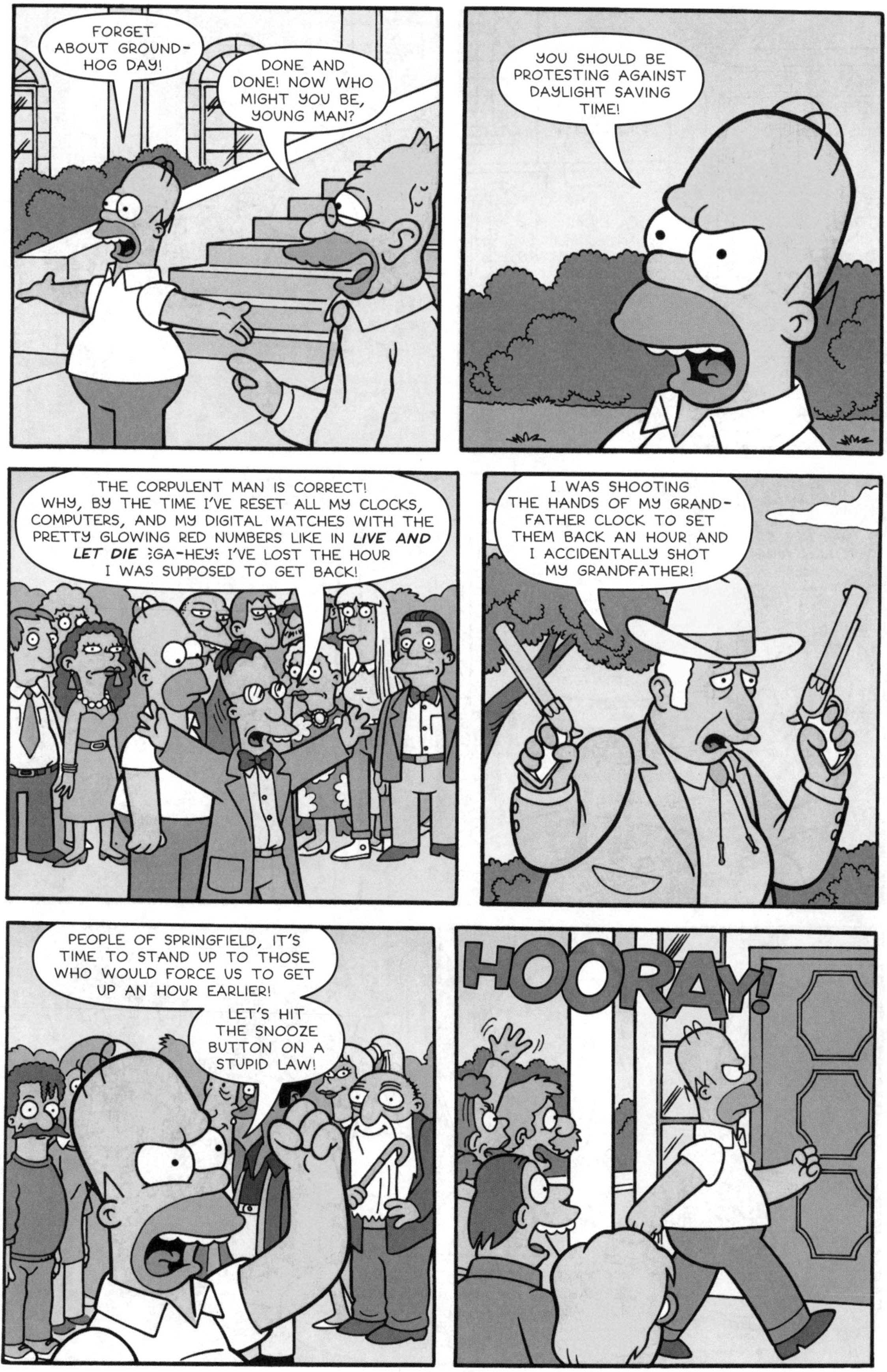
FORGET ABOUT GROUND-HOG DAY!
DONE AND DONE! NOW WHO MIGHT YOU BE, YOUNG MAN?
YOU SHOULD BE PROTESTING AGAINST DAYLIGHT SAVING TIME!
THE CORPULENT MAN IS CORRECT! WHY, BY THE TIME I'VE RESET ALL MY CLOCKS, COMPUTERS, AND MY DIGITAL WATCHES WITH THE PRETTY GLOWING RED NUMBERS LIKE IN LIVE AND LET DIE ;GA-HEY; I'VE LOST THE HOUR I WAS SUPPOSED TO GET BACK!
I WAS SHOOTING THE HANDS OF MY GRAND-FATHER CLOCK TO SET THEM BACK AN HOUR AND I ACCIDENTALLY SHOT MY GRANDFATHER!
PEOPLE OF SPRINGFIELD, IT'S TIME TO STAND UP TO THOSE WHO WOULD FORCE US TO GET UP AN HOUR EARLIER!
LET'S HIT THE SNOOZE BUTTON ON A STUPID LAW!
HOORAY!

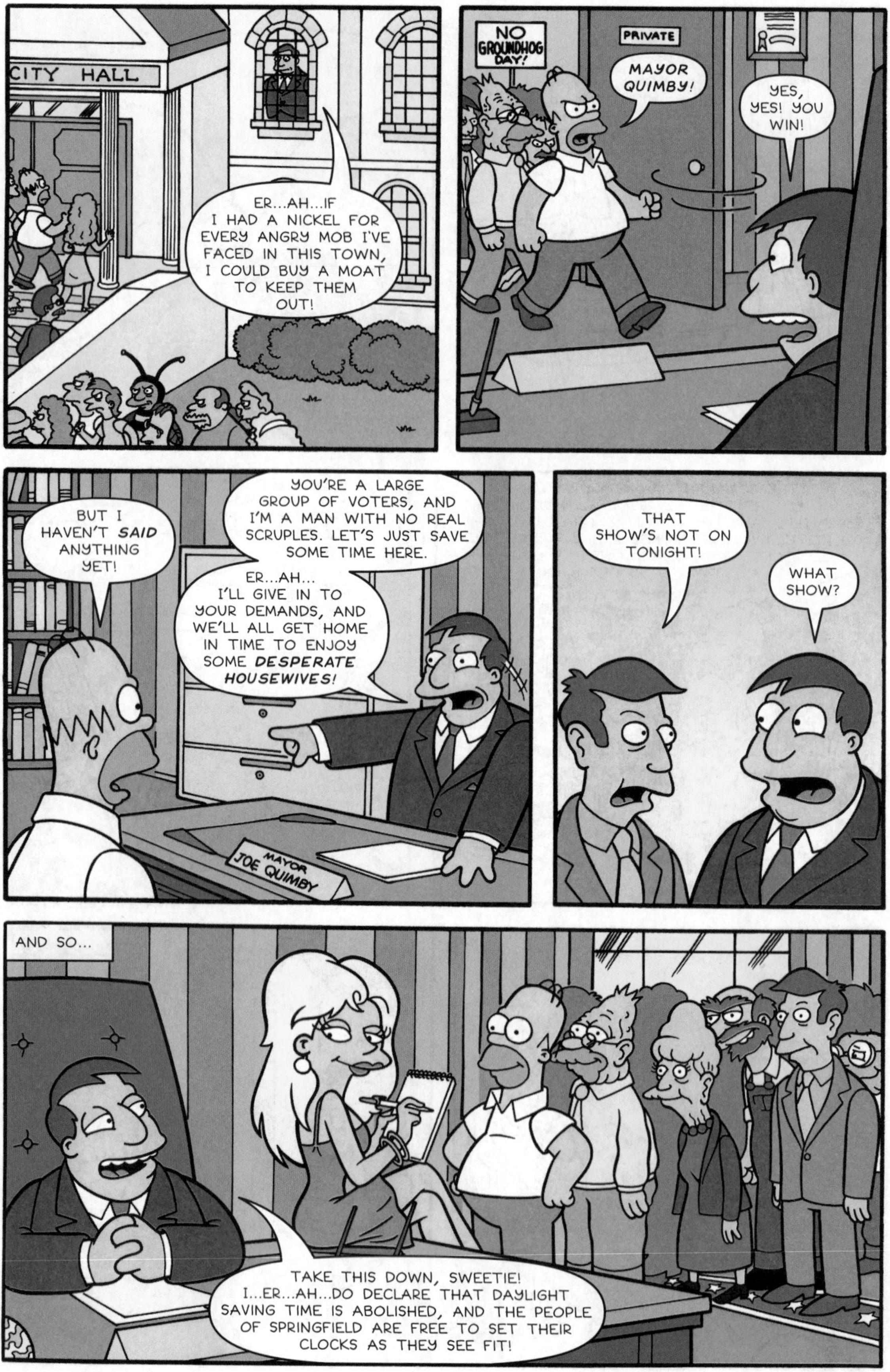
CITY HALL
ER...AH...IF I HAD A NICKEL FOR EVERY ANGRY MOB I'VE FACED IN THIS TOWN, I COULD BUY A MOAT TO KEEP THEM OUT!
NO GROUNDHOG DAY!
PRIVATE
MAYOR QUIMBY!
YES, YES! YOU WIN!
BUT I HAVEN'T SAID ANYTHING YET!
YOU'RE A LARGE GROUP OF VOTERS, AND I'M A MAN WITH NO REAL SCRUPLES. LET'S JUST SAVE SOME TIME HERE.
ER...AH... I'LL GIVE IN TO YOUR DEMANDS, AND WE'LL ALL GET HOME IN TIME TO ENJOY SOME DESPERATE HOUSEWIVES!
MAYOR JOE QUIMBY
THAT SHOW'S NOT ON TONIGHT!
WHAT SHOW?
AND SO...
TAKE THIS DOWN, SWEETIE! I...ER...AH...DO DECLARE THAT DAYLIGHT SAVING TIME IS ABOLISHED, AND THE PEOPLE OF SPRINGFIELD ARE FREE TO SET THEIR CLOCKS AS THEY SEE FIT!

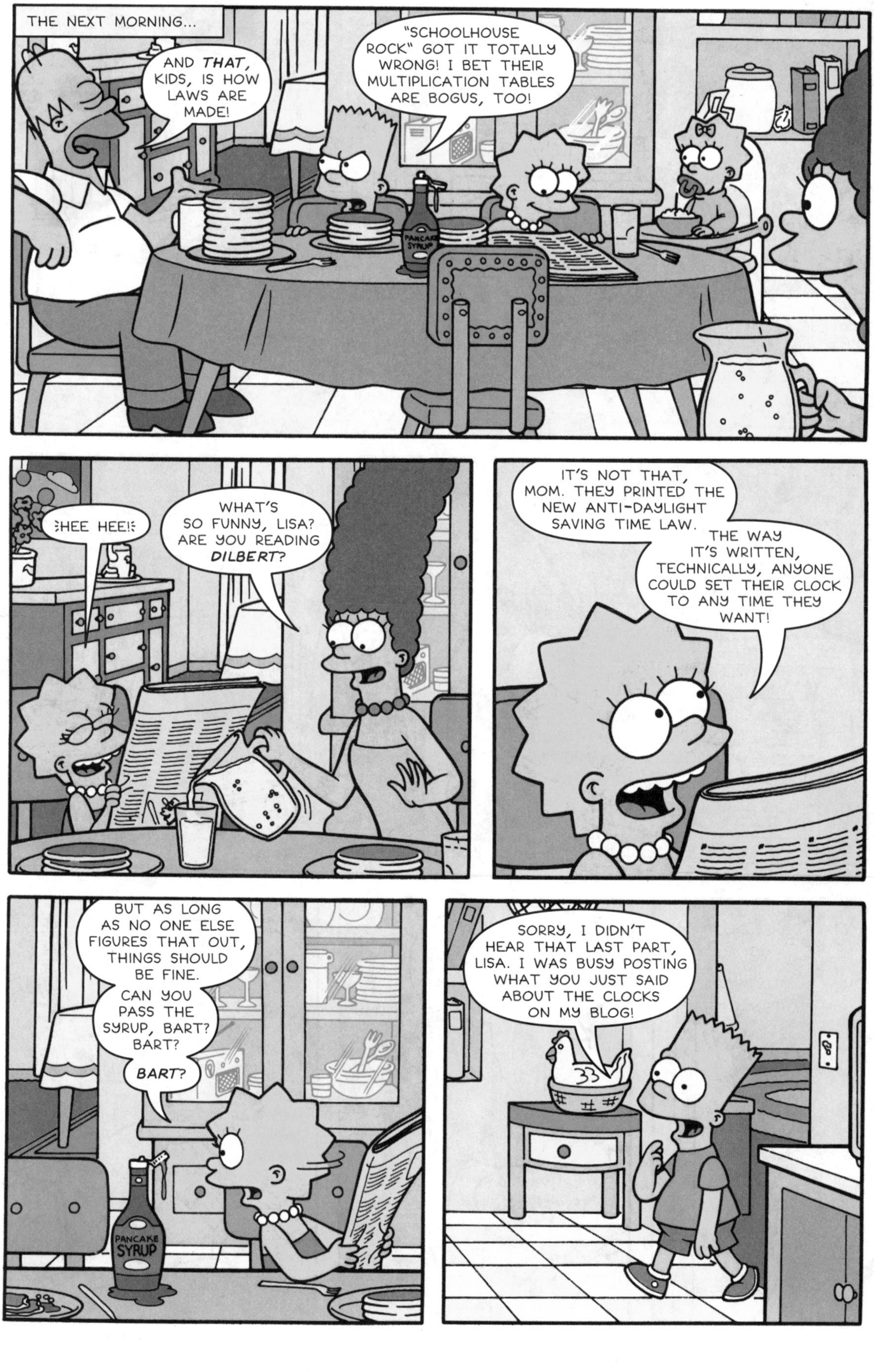
THE NEXT MORNING...
AND *THAT*, KIDS, IS HOW LAWS ARE MADE!
"SCHOOLHOUSE ROCK" GOT IT TOTALLY WRONG! I BET THEIR MULTIPLICATION TABLES ARE BOGUS, TOO!
PANCAKE SYRUP
HEE HEE!
WHAT'S SO FUNNY, LISA? ARE YOU READING *DILBERT*?
IT'S NOT THAT, MOM. THEY PRINTED THE NEW ANTI-DAYLIGHT SAVING TIME LAW.
THE WAY IT'S WRITTEN, TECHNICALLY, ANYONE COULD SET THEIR CLOCK TO ANY TIME THEY WANT!
BUT AS LONG AS NO ONE ELSE FIGURES THAT OUT, THINGS SHOULD BE FINE.
CAN YOU PASS THE SYRUP, BART? BART?
BART?
PANCAKE SYRUP
SORRY, I DIDN'T HEAR THAT LAST PART, LISA. I WAS BUSY POSTING WHAT YOU JUST SAID ABOUT THE CLOCKS ON MY BLOG!

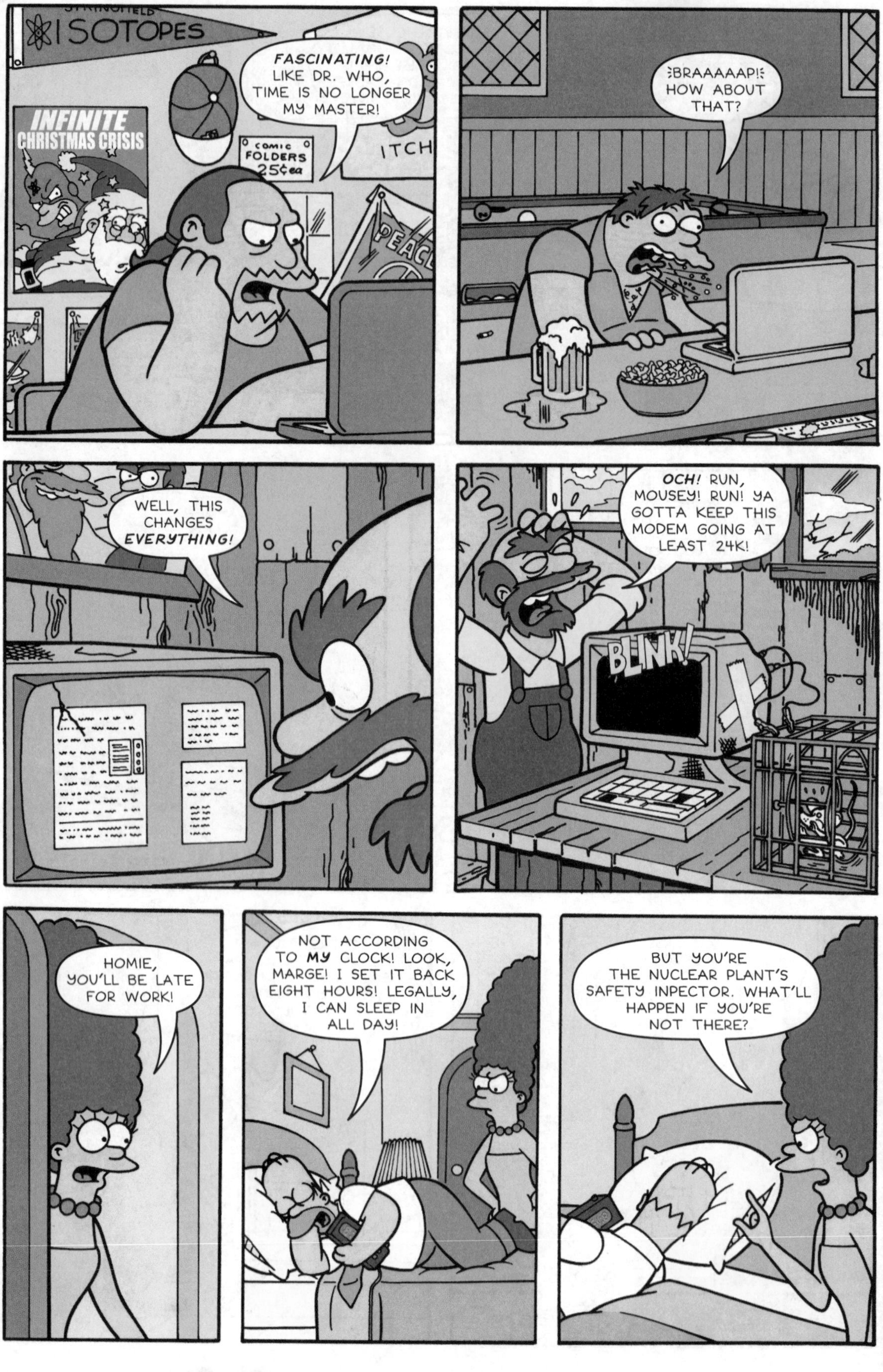
SPRINGFIELD ISOTOPES
INFINITE CHRISTMAS CRISIS
COMIC FOLDERS 25¢ea
ITCH
PEACE
FASCINATING! LIKE DR. WHO, TIME IS NO LONGER MY MASTER!
BRAAAAAP! HOW ABOUT THAT?
WELL, THIS CHANGES EVERYTHING!
OCH! RUN, MOUSEY! RUN! YA GOTTA KEEP THIS MODEM GOING AT LEAST 24K!
BLINK!
HOMIE, YOU'LL BE LATE FOR WORK!
NOT ACCORDING TO MY CLOCK! LOOK, MARGE! I SET IT BACK EIGHT HOURS! LEGALLY, I CAN SLEEP IN ALL DAY!
BUT YOU'RE THE NUCLEAR PLANT'S SAFETY INPECTOR. WHAT'LL HAPPEN IF YOU'RE NOT THERE?

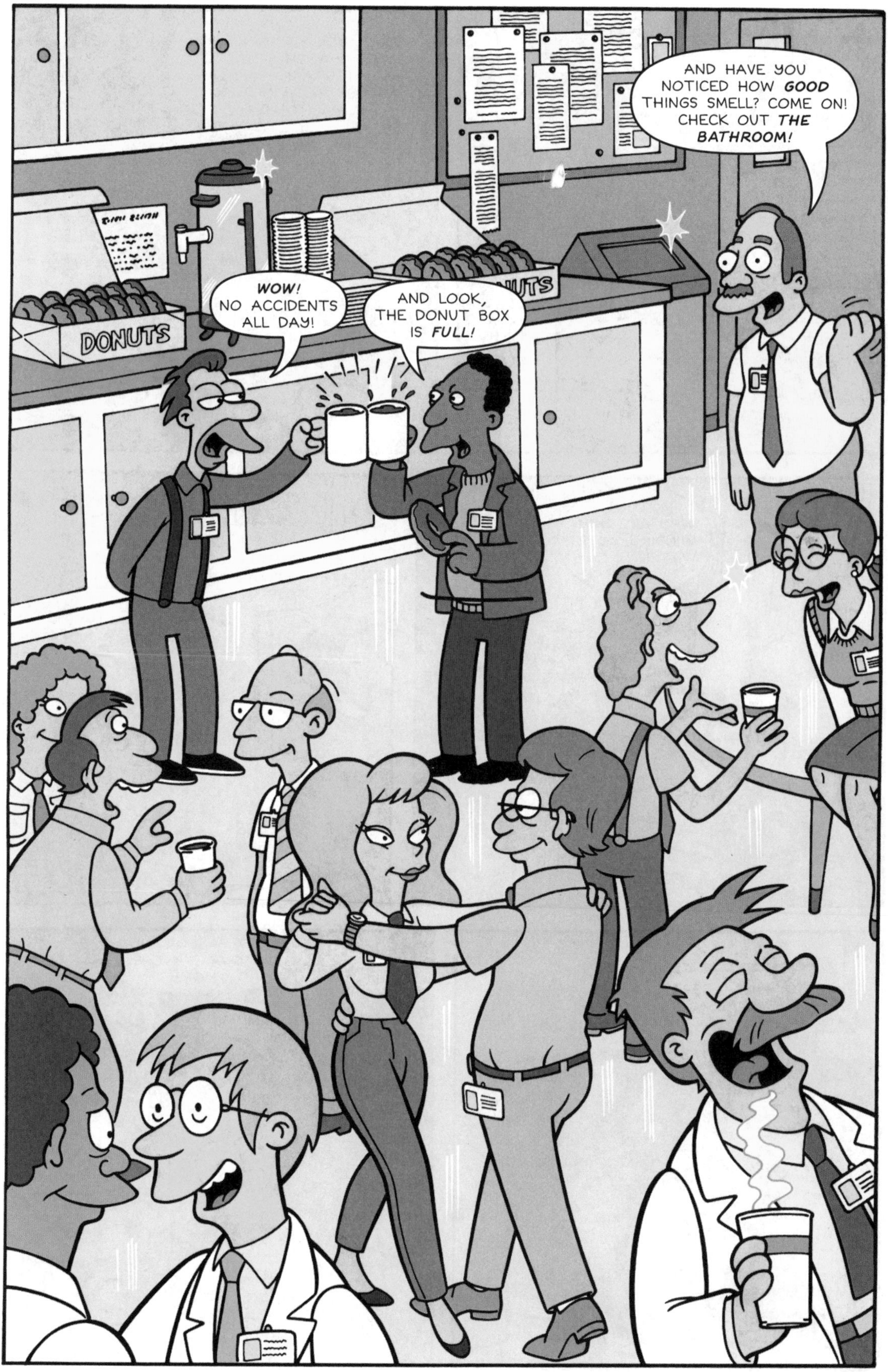
WOW! NO ACCIDENTS ALL DAY!
AND LOOK, THE DONUT BOX IS FULL!
AND HAVE YOU NOTICED HOW GOOD THINGS SMELL? COME ON! CHECK OUT THE BATHROOM!
DONUTS

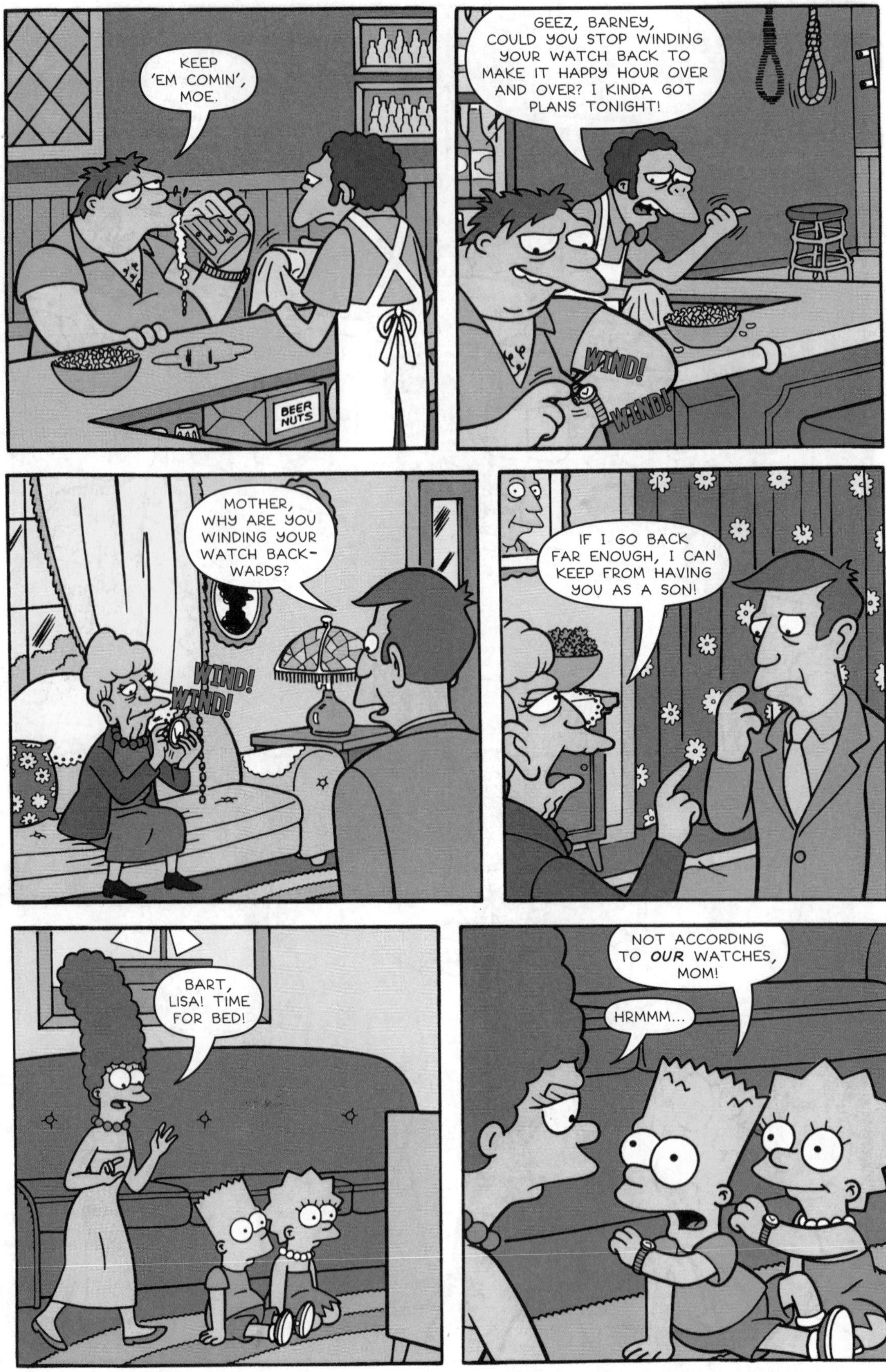
KEEP 'EM COMIN', MOE.
GEEZ, BARNEY, COULD YOU STOP WINDING YOUR WATCH BACK TO MAKE IT HAPPY HOUR OVER AND OVER? I KINDA GOT PLANS TONIGHT!
WIND!
WIND!
BEER NUTS
MOTHER, WHY ARE YOU WINDING YOUR WATCH BACK-WARDS?
WIND!
WIND!
IF I GO BACK FAR ENOUGH, I CAN KEEP FROM HAVING YOU AS A SON!
BART, LISA! TIME FOR BED!
NOT ACCORDING TO *OUR* WATCHES, MOM!
HRMMM...

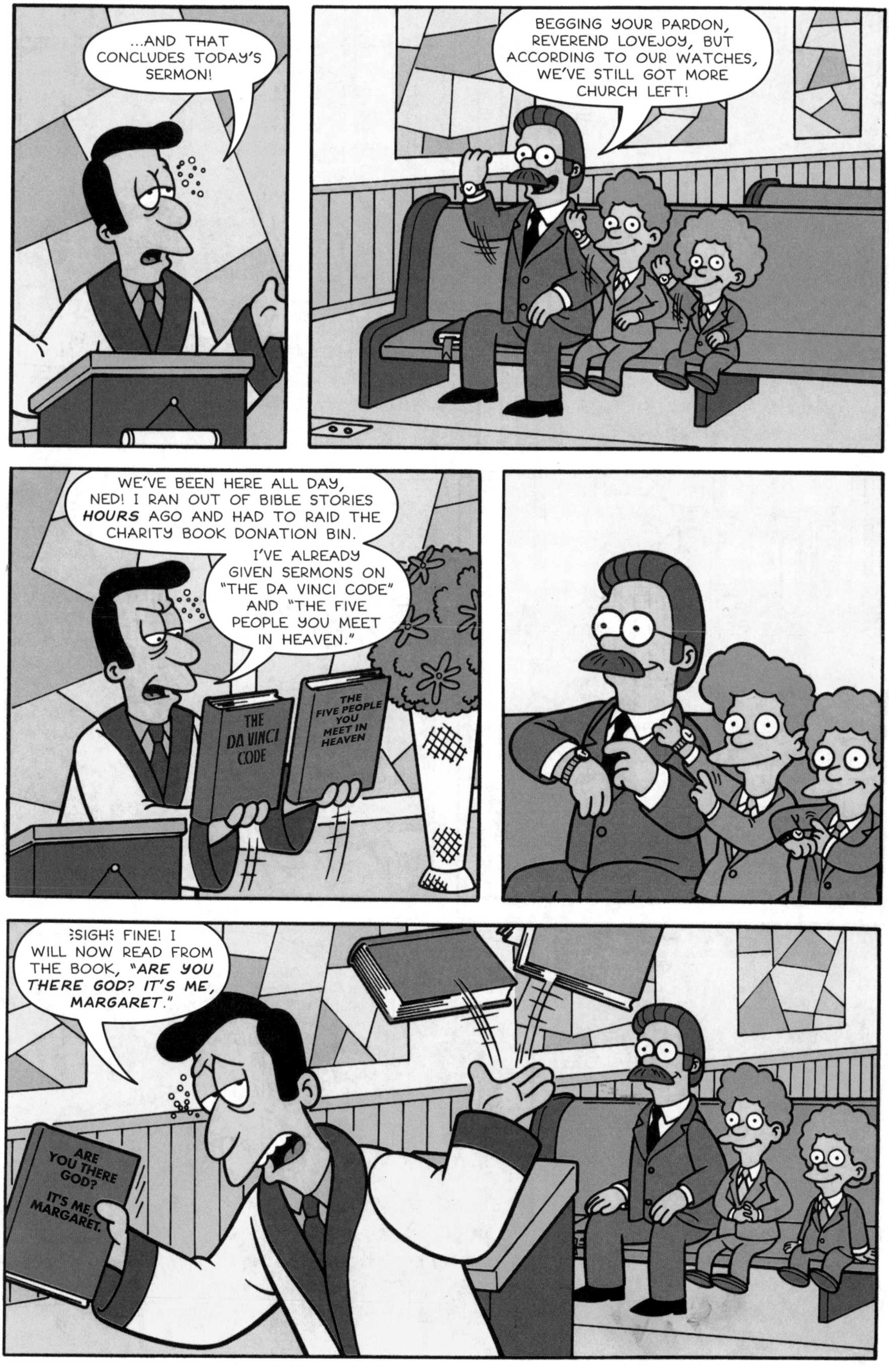
...AND THAT CONCLUDES TODAY'S SERMON!
BEGGING YOUR PARDON, REVEREND LOVEJOY, BUT ACCORDING TO OUR WATCHES, WE'VE STILL GOT MORE CHURCH LEFT!
WE'VE BEEN HERE ALL DAY, NED! I RAN OUT OF BIBLE STORIES HOURS AGO AND HAD TO RAID THE CHARITY BOOK DONATION BIN.
I'VE ALREADY GIVEN SERMONS ON "THE DA VINCI CODE" AND "THE FIVE PEOPLE YOU MEET IN HEAVEN."
THE DA VINCI CODE
THE FIVE PEOPLE YOU MEET IN HEAVEN
:SIGH: FINE! I WILL NOW READ FROM THE BOOK, "ARE YOU THERE GOD? IT'S ME, MARGARET."
ARE YOU THERE GOD? IT'S ME, MARGARET.

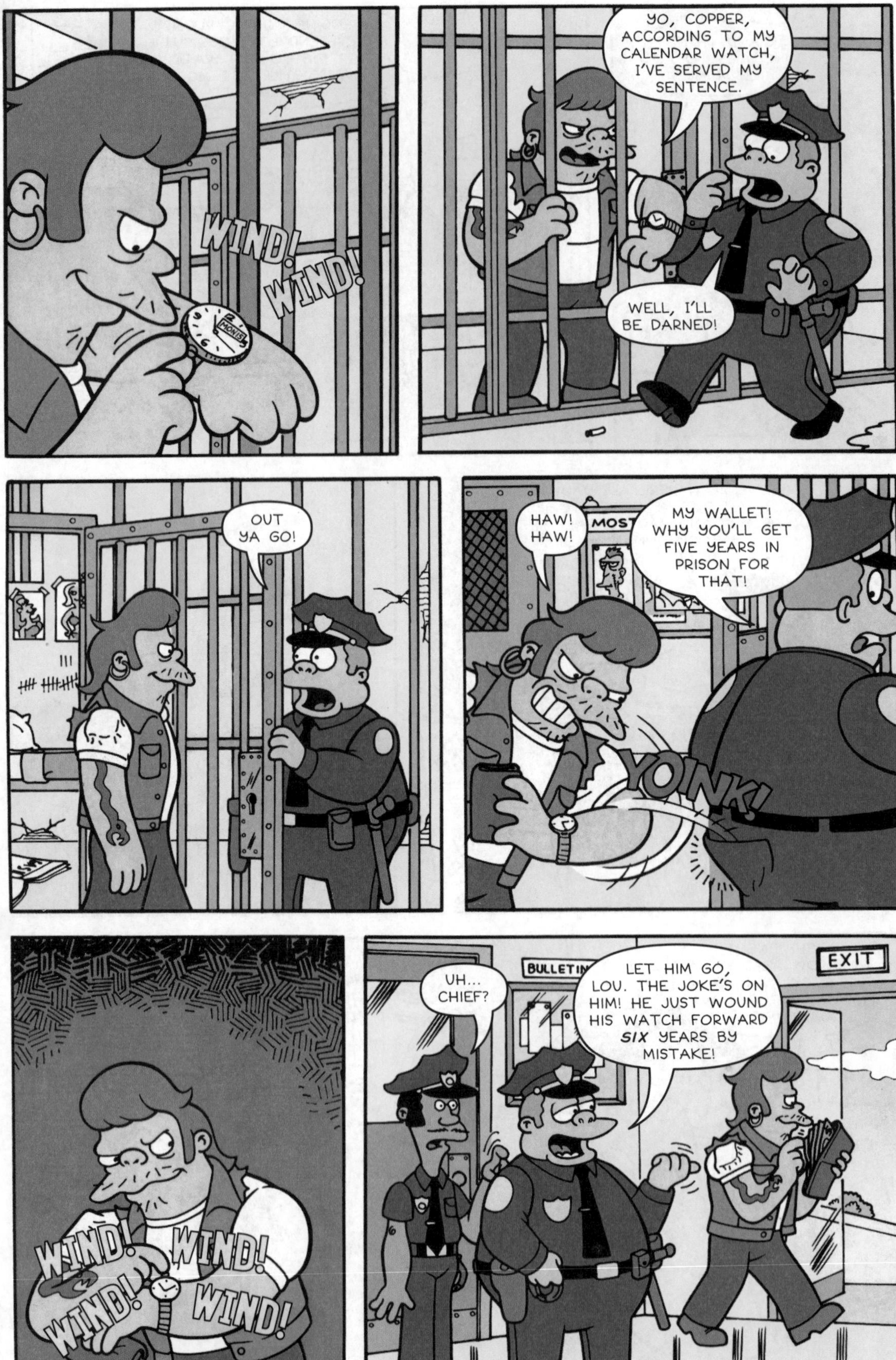
WIND! WIND!
MONIS
YO, COPPER, ACCORDING TO MY CALENDAR WATCH, I'VE SERVED MY SENTENCE.
WELL, I'LL BE DARNED!
OUT YA GO!
HAW! HAW!
MOST
MY WALLET! WHY YOU'LL GET FIVE YEARS IN PRISON FOR THAT!
YOINK!
WIND! WIND! WIND! WIND!
BULLETIN
EXIT
UH... CHIEF?
LET HIM GO, LOU. THE JOKE'S ON HIM! HE JUST WOUND HIS WATCH FORWARD *SIX* YEARS BY MISTAKE!

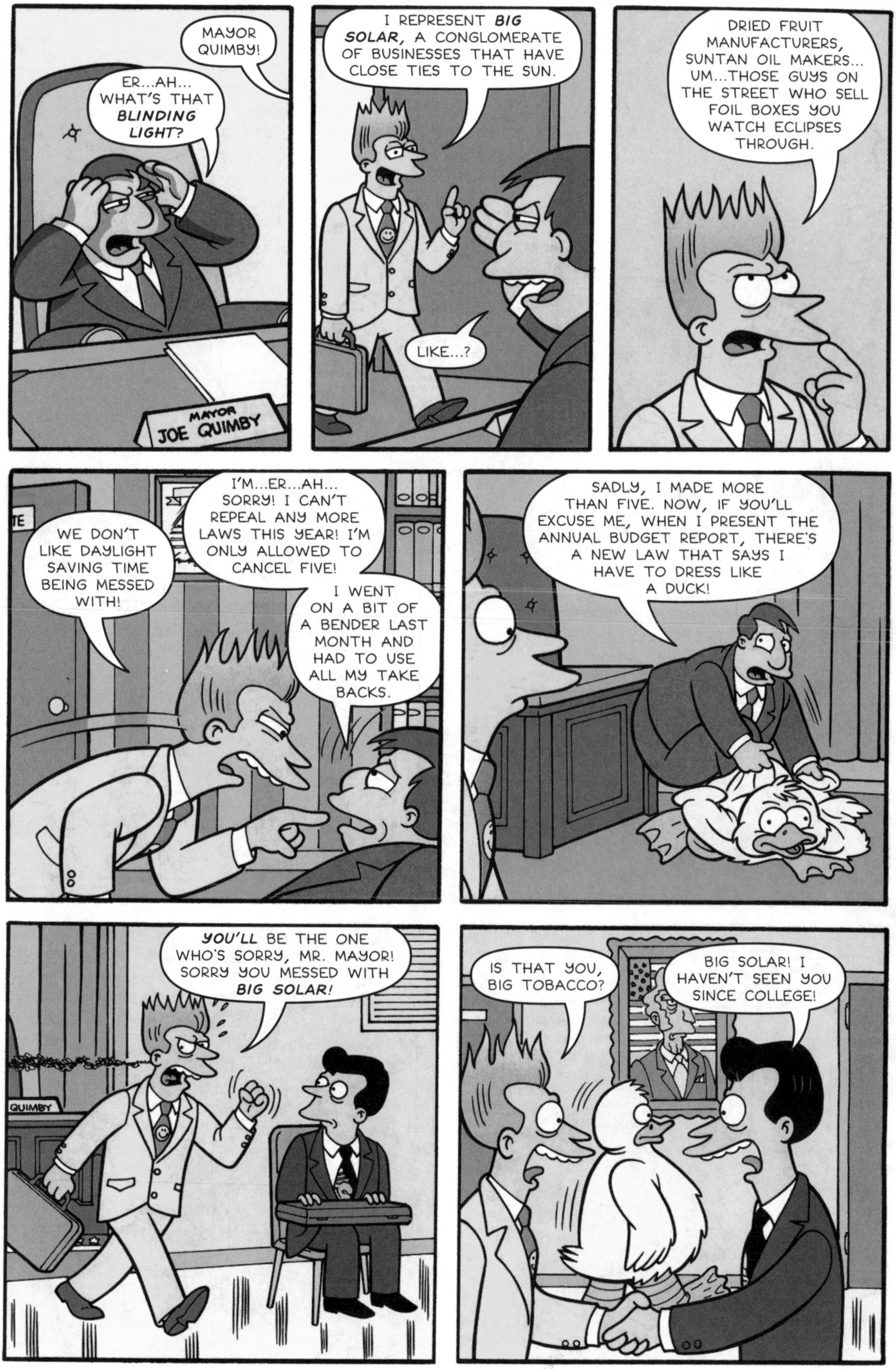
MAYOR QUIMBY!
ER...AH... WHAT'S THAT BLINDING LIGHT?
MAYOR JOE QUIMBY
I REPRESENT BIG SOLAR, A CONGLOMERATE OF BUSINESSES THAT HAVE CLOSE TIES TO THE SUN.
LIKE...?
DRIED FRUIT MANUFACTURERS, SUNTAN OIL MAKERS... UM...THOSE GUYS ON THE STREET WHO SELL FOIL BOXES YOU WATCH ECLIPSES THROUGH.
WE DON'T LIKE DAYLIGHT SAVING TIME BEING MESSED WITH!
I'M...ER...AH... SORRY! I CAN'T REPEAL ANY MORE LAWS THIS YEAR! I'M ONLY ALLOWED TO CANCEL FIVE!
I WENT ON A BIT OF A BENDER LAST MONTH AND HAD TO USE ALL MY TAKE BACKS.
SADLY, I MADE MORE THAN FIVE. NOW, IF YOU'LL EXCUSE ME, WHEN I PRESENT THE ANNUAL BUDGET REPORT, THERE'S A NEW LAW THAT SAYS I HAVE TO DRESS LIKE A DUCK!
YOU'LL BE THE ONE WHO'S SORRY, MR. MAYOR! SORRY YOU MESSED WITH BIG SOLAR!
QUIMBY
IS THAT YOU, BIG TOBACCO?
BIG SOLAR! I HAVEN'T SEEN YOU SINCE COLLEGE!

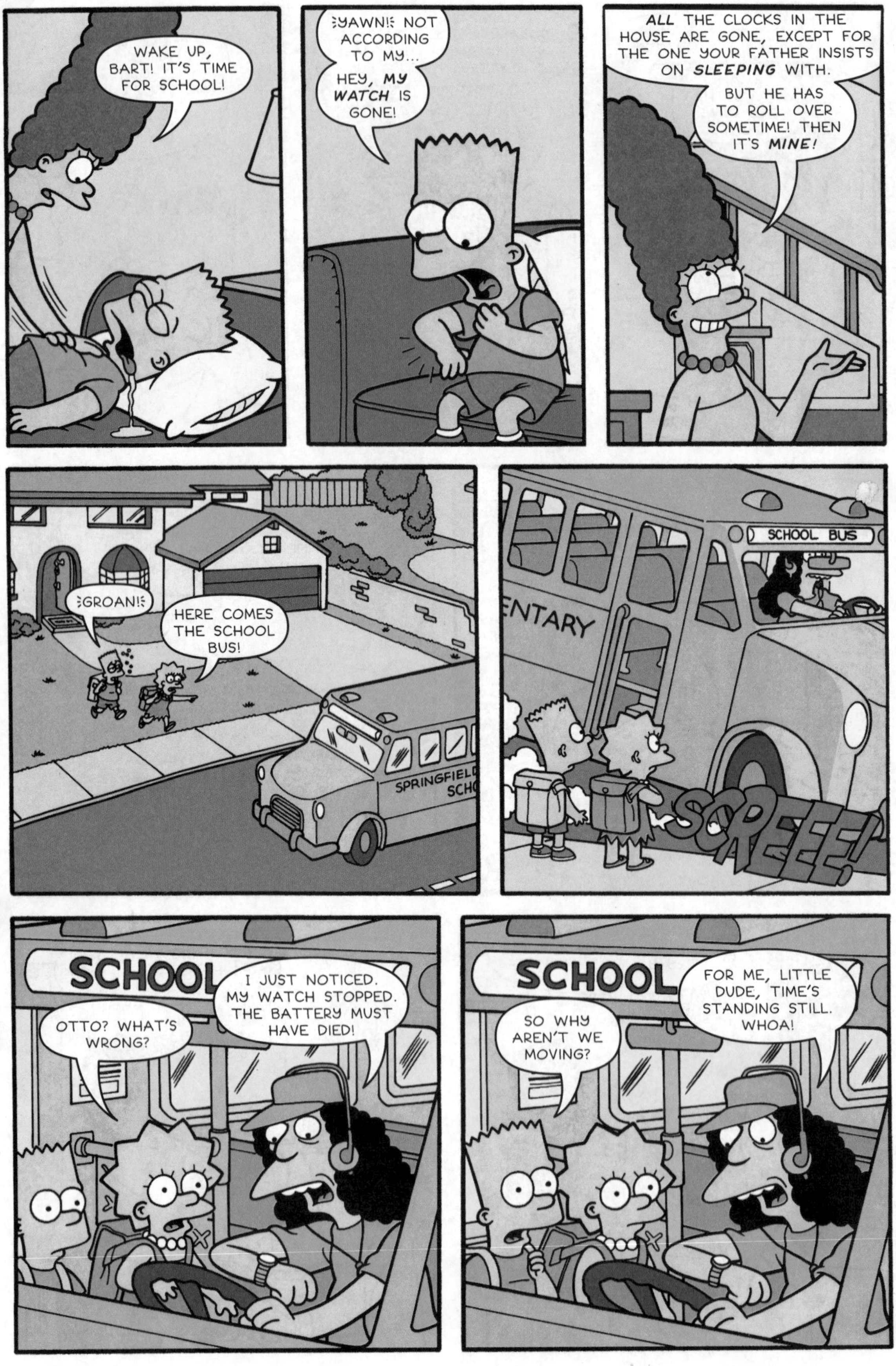
WAKE UP, BART! IT'S TIME FOR SCHOOL!
⁒YAWN!⁒ NOT ACCORDING TO MY...
HEY, MY WATCH IS GONE!
ALL THE CLOCKS IN THE HOUSE ARE GONE, EXCEPT FOR THE ONE YOUR FATHER INSISTS ON SLEEPING WITH.
BUT HE HAS TO ROLL OVER SOMETIME! THEN IT'S MINE!
⁒GROAN!⁒
HERE COMES THE SCHOOL BUS!
SPRINGFIELD SCHO
SCHOOL BUS
ENTARY
SCREEE!
SCHOOL
OTTO? WHAT'S WRONG?
I JUST NOTICED. MY WATCH STOPPED. THE BATTERY MUST HAVE DIED!
SCHOOL
SO WHY AREN'T WE MOVING?
FOR ME, LITTLE DUDE, TIME'S STANDING STILL. WHOA!

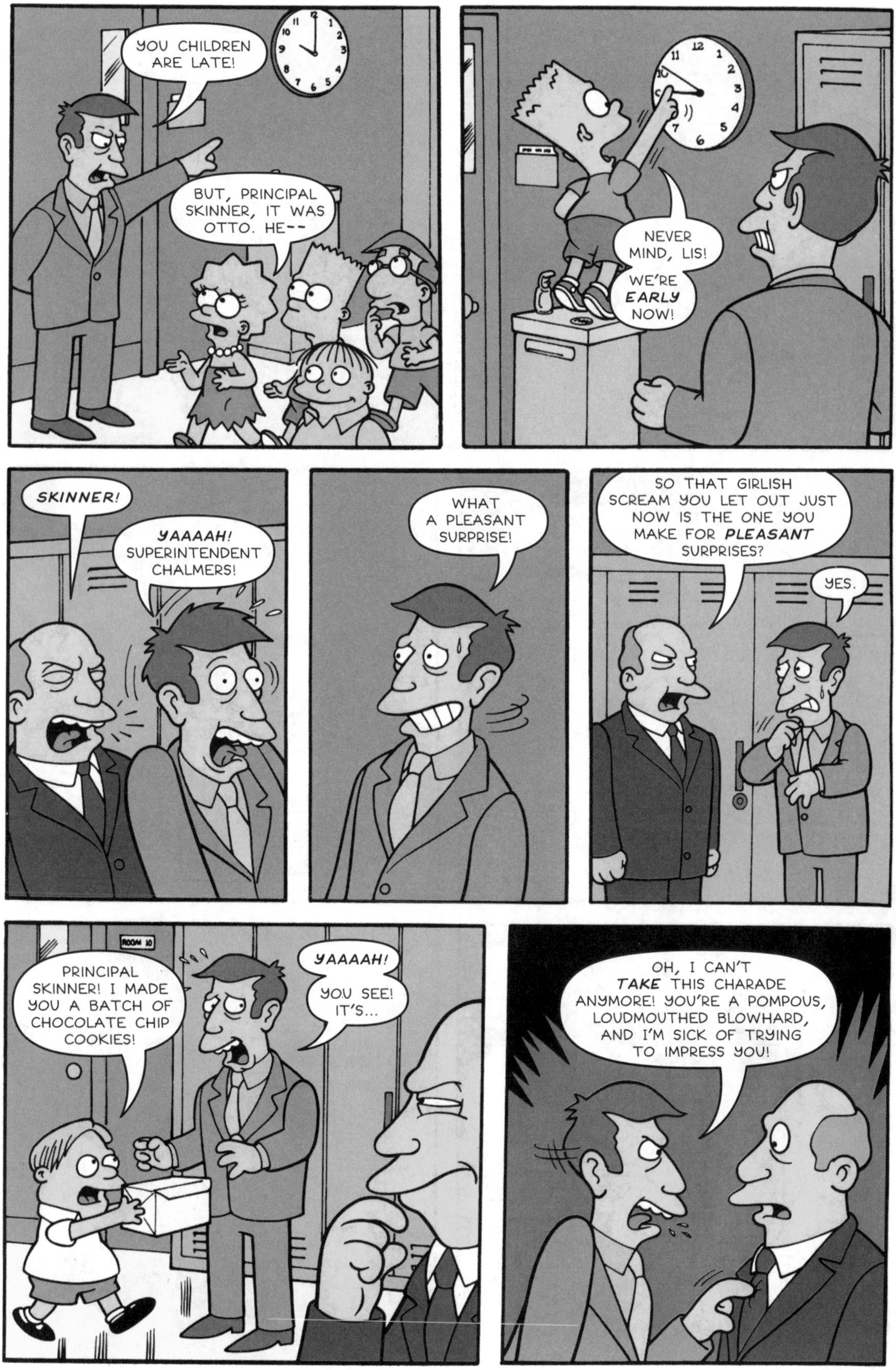
YOU CHILDREN ARE LATE!
BUT, PRINCIPAL SKINNER, IT WAS OTTO. HE--
NEVER MIND, LIS!
WE'RE EARLY NOW!
SKINNER!
YAAAAH! SUPERINTENDENT CHALMERS!
WHAT A PLEASANT SURPRISE!
SO THAT GIRLISH SCREAM YOU LET OUT JUST NOW IS THE ONE YOU MAKE FOR PLEASANT SURPRISES?
YES.
ROOM 10
PRINCIPAL SKINNER! I MADE YOU A BATCH OF CHOCOLATE CHIP COOKIES!
YAAAAH!
YOU SEE! IT'S...
OH, I CAN'T TAKE THIS CHARADE ANYMORE! YOU'RE A POMPOUS, LOUDMOUTHED BLOWHARD, AND I'M SICK OF TRYING TO IMPRESS YOU!

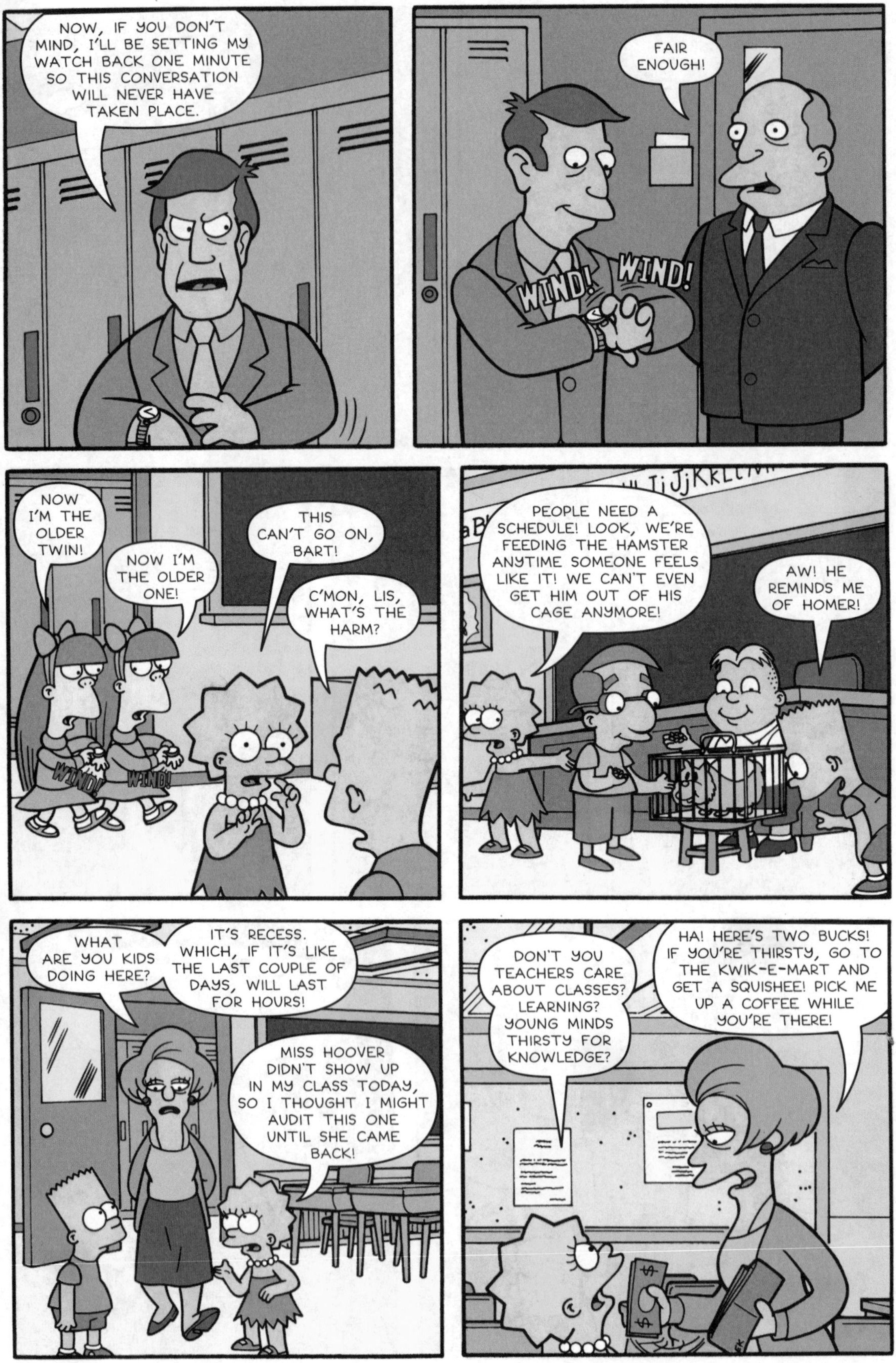
NOW, IF YOU DON'T MIND, I'LL BE SETTING MY WATCH BACK ONE MINUTE SO THIS CONVERSATION WILL NEVER HAVE TAKEN PLACE.
FAIR ENOUGH!
WIND!
WIND!
NOW I'M THE OLDER TWIN!
NOW I'M THE OLDER ONE!
WIND!
WIND!
THIS CAN'T GO ON, BART!
C'MON, LIS, WHAT'S THE HARM?
PEOPLE NEED A SCHEDULE! LOOK, WE'RE FEEDING THE HAMSTER ANYTIME SOMEONE FEELS LIKE IT! WE CAN'T EVEN GET HIM OUT OF HIS CAGE ANYMORE!
AW! HE REMINDS ME OF HOMER!
WHAT ARE YOU KIDS DOING HERE?
IT'S RECESS. WHICH, IF IT'S LIKE THE LAST COUPLE OF DAYS, WILL LAST FOR HOURS!
MISS HOOVER DIDN'T SHOW UP IN MY CLASS TODAY, SO I THOUGHT I MIGHT AUDIT THIS ONE UNTIL SHE CAME BACK!
DON'T YOU TEACHERS CARE ABOUT CLASSES? LEARNING? YOUNG MINDS THIRSTY FOR KNOWLEDGE?
HA! HERE'S TWO BUCKS! IF YOU'RE THIRSTY, GO TO THE KWIK-E-MART AND GET A SQUISHEE! PICK ME UP A COFFEE WHILE YOU'RE THERE!

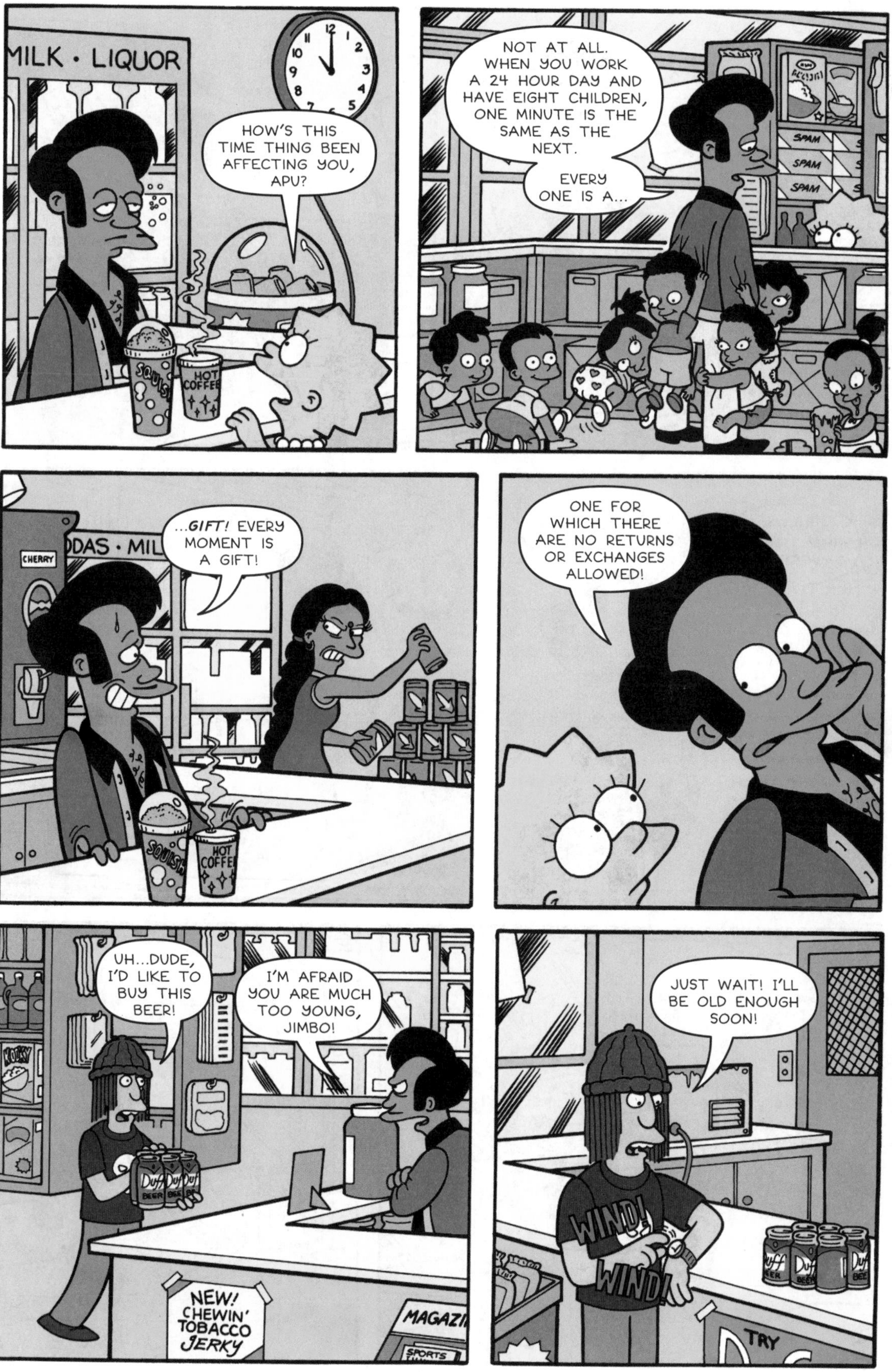
MILK • LIQUOR
HOW'S THIS TIME THING BEEN AFFECTING YOU, APU?
NOT AT ALL. WHEN YOU WORK A 24 HOUR DAY AND HAVE EIGHT CHILDREN, ONE MINUTE IS THE SAME AS THE NEXT.
EVERY ONE IS A...
SPAM
SPAM
SPAM
CHERRY
...GIFT! EVERY MOMENT IS A GIFT!
ONE FOR WHICH THERE ARE NO RETURNS OR EXCHANGES ALLOWED!
UH...DUDE, I'D LIKE TO BUY THIS BEER!
I'M AFRAID YOU ARE MUCH TOO YOUNG, JIMBO!
NEW! CHEWIN' TOBACCO JERKY
JUST WAIT! I'LL BE OLD ENOUGH SOON!
WIND!
WIND!
TRY

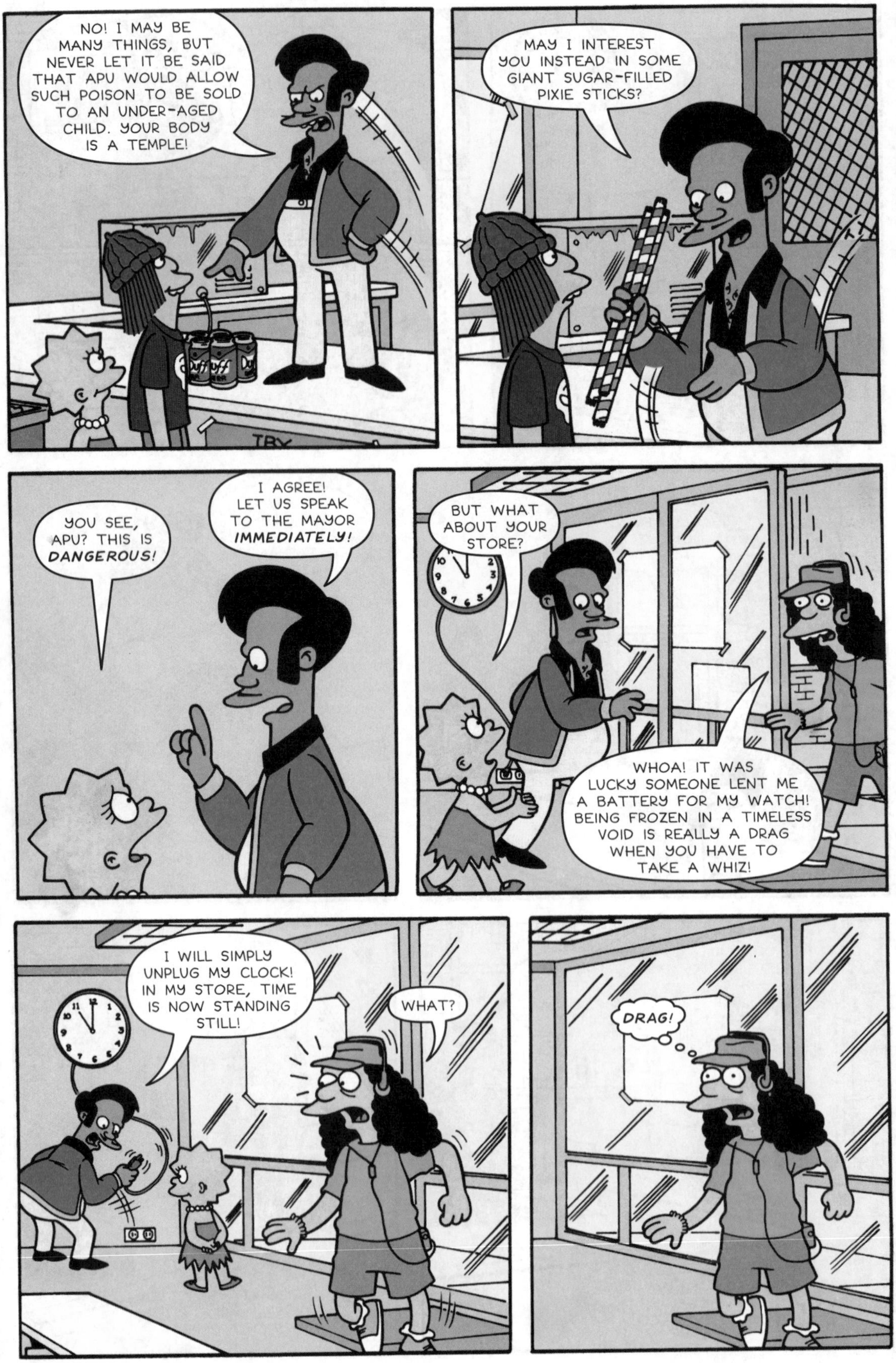
NO! I MAY BE MANY THINGS, BUT NEVER LET IT BE SAID THAT APU WOULD ALLOW SUCH POISON TO BE SOLD TO AN UNDER-AGED CHILD. YOUR BODY IS A TEMPLE!
MAY I INTEREST YOU INSTEAD IN SOME GIANT SUGAR-FILLED PIXIE STICKS?
YOU SEE, APU? THIS IS DANGEROUS!
I AGREE! LET US SPEAK TO THE MAYOR IMMEDIATELY!
BUT WHAT ABOUT YOUR STORE?
WHOA! IT WAS LUCKY SOMEONE LENT ME A BATTERY FOR MY WATCH! BEING FROZEN IN A TIMELESS VOID IS REALLY A DRAG WHEN YOU HAVE TO TAKE A WHIZ!
I WILL SIMPLY UNPLUG MY CLOCK! IN MY STORE, TIME IS NOW STANDING STILL!
WHAT?
DRAG!

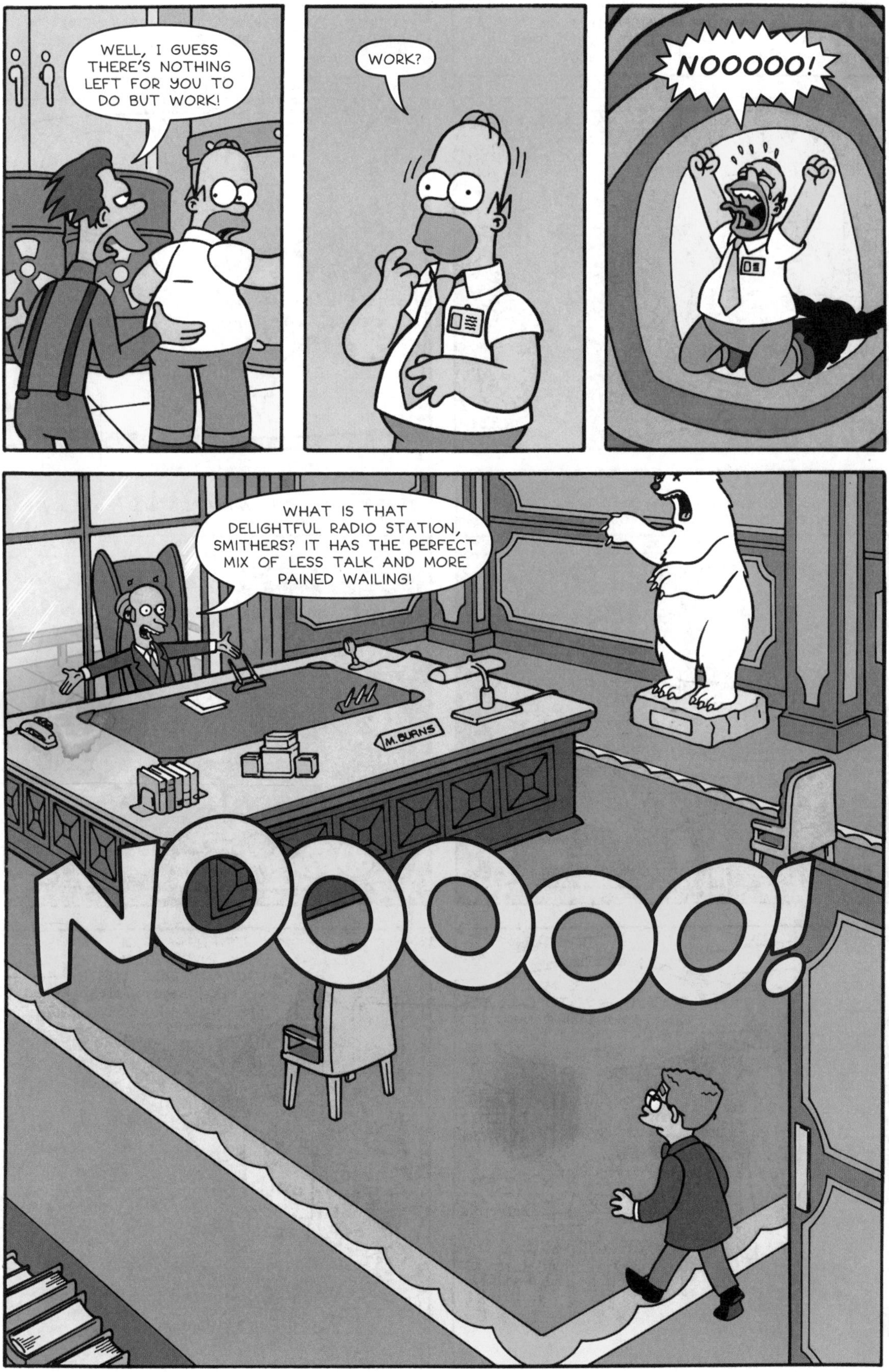

WELL, I GUESS THERE'S NOTHING LEFT FOR YOU TO DO BUT WORK!
WORK?
NOOOOO!
WHAT IS THAT DELIGHTFUL RADIO STATION, SMITHERS? IT HAS THE PERFECT MIX OF LESS TALK AND MORE PAINED WAILING!
M. BURNS
NOOOOO!

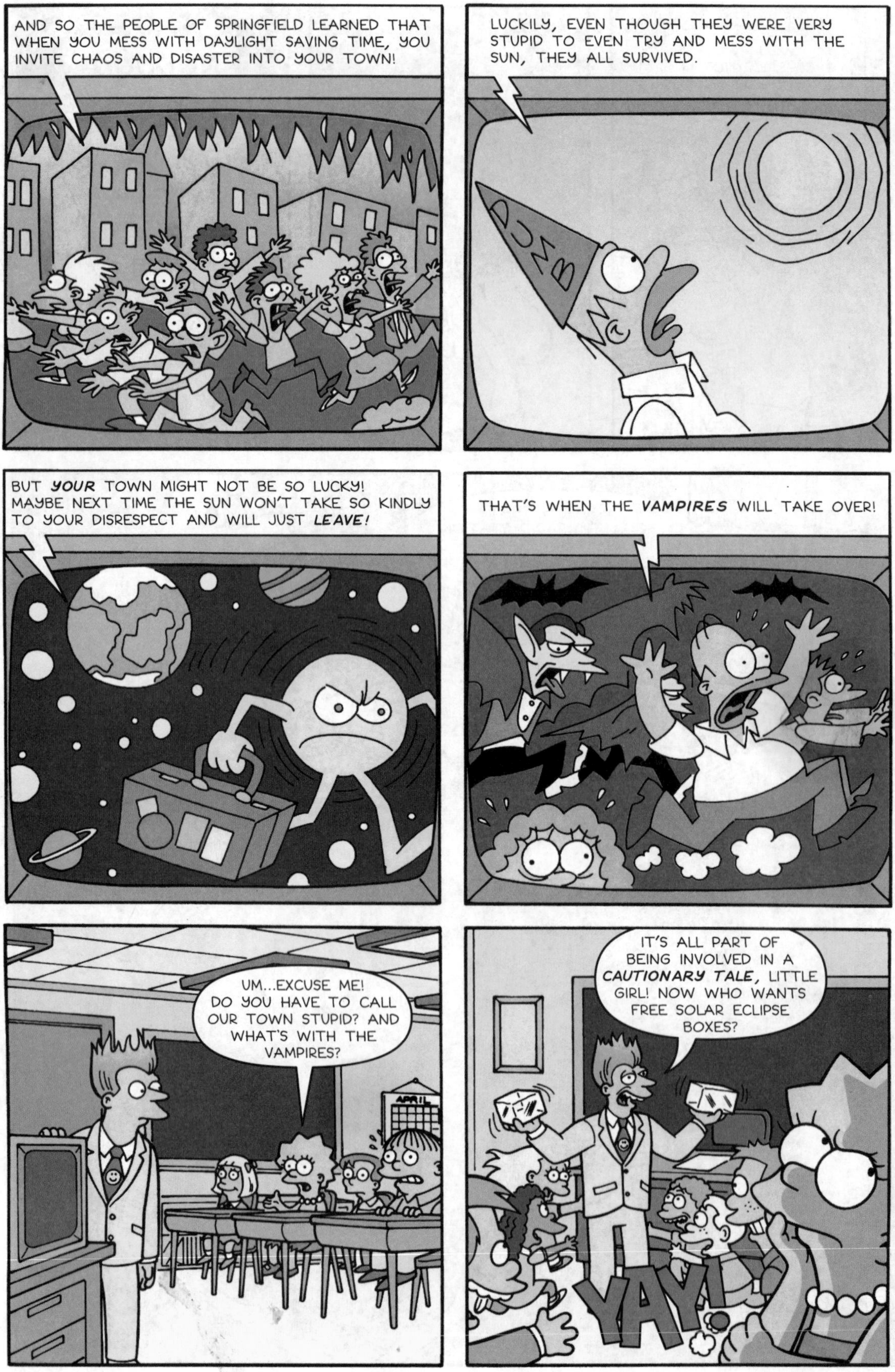
AND SO THE PEOPLE OF SPRINGFIELD LEARNED THAT WHEN YOU MESS WITH DAYLIGHT SAVING TIME, YOU INVITE CHAOS AND DISASTER INTO YOUR TOWN!
LUCKILY, EVEN THOUGH THEY WERE VERY STUPID TO EVEN TRY AND MESS WITH THE SUN, THEY ALL SURVIVED.
BUT YOUR TOWN MIGHT NOT BE SO LUCKY! MAYBE NEXT TIME THE SUN WON'T TAKE SO KINDLY TO YOUR DISRESPECT AND WILL JUST LEAVE!
THAT'S WHEN THE VAMPIRES WILL TAKE OVER!
UM...EXCUSE ME! DO YOU HAVE TO CALL OUR TOWN STUPID? AND WHAT'S WITH THE VAMPIRES?
APRIL
IT'S ALL PART OF BEING INVOLVED IN A CAUTIONARY TALE, LITTLE GIRL! NOW WHO WANTS FREE SOLAR ECLIPSE BOXES?
YAY!

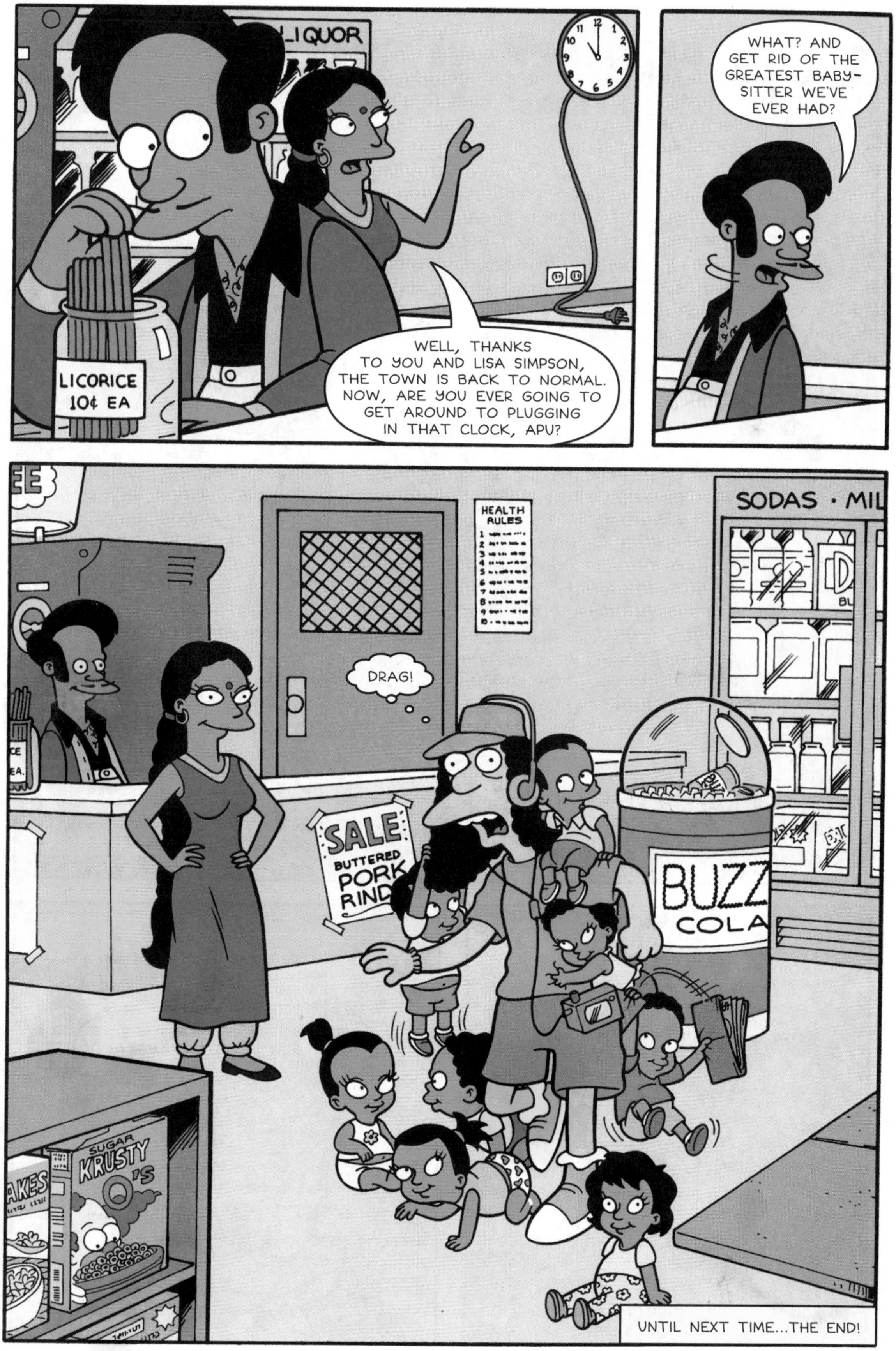
LIQUOR
LICORICE 10¢ EA
WELL, THANKS TO YOU AND LISA SIMPSON, THE TOWN IS BACK TO NORMAL. NOW, ARE YOU EVER GOING TO GET AROUND TO PLUGGING IN THAT CLOCK, APU?
WHAT? AND GET RID OF THE GREATEST BABY-SITTER WE'VE EVER HAD?
SODAS · MIL
HEALTH RULES
DRAG!
SALE BUTTERED PORK RIND
BUZZ COLA
SUGAR KRUSTY O'S
UNTIL NEXT TIME...THE END!

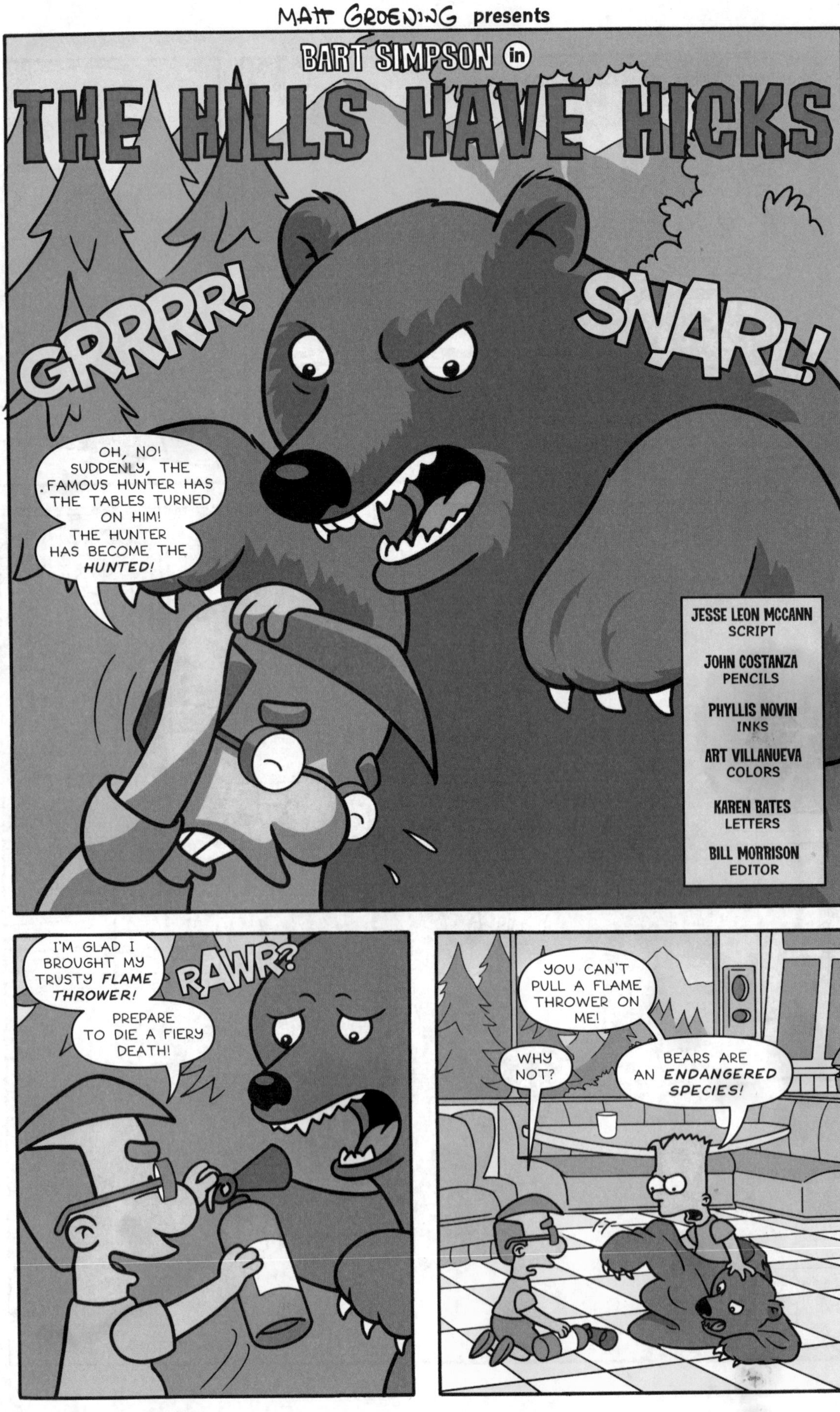
MATT GROENING presents
BART SIMPSON in
THE HILLS HAVE HICKS
GRRRR!
SNARL!
OH, NO! SUDDENLY, THE FAMOUS HUNTER HAS THE TABLES TURNED ON HIM!
THE HUNTER HAS BECOME THE HUNTED!
JESSE LEON MCCANN SCRIPT
JOHN COSTANZA PENCILS
PHYLLIS NOVIN INKS
ART VILLANUEVA COLORS
KAREN BATES LETTERS
BILL MORRISON EDITOR
I'M GLAD I BROUGHT MY TRUSTY FLAME THROWER!
PREPARE TO DIE A FIERY DEATH!
RAWR?
YOU CAN'T PULL A FLAME THROWER ON ME!
WHY NOT?
BEARS ARE AN ENDANGERED SPECIES!

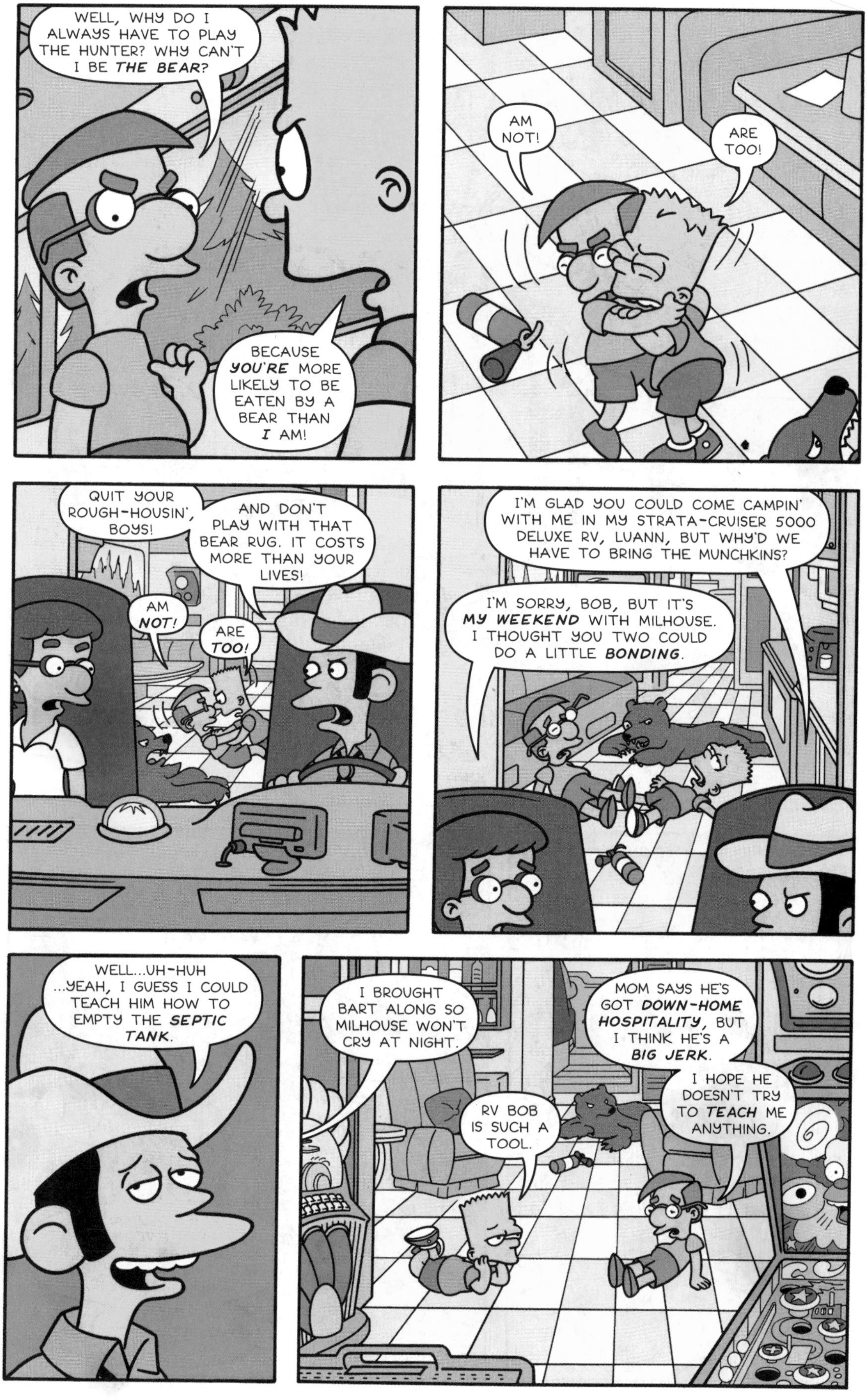
WELL, WHY DO I ALWAYS HAVE TO PLAY THE HUNTER? WHY CAN'T I BE THE BEAR?
BECAUSE YOU'RE MORE LIKELY TO BE EATEN BY A BEAR THAN I AM!
AM NOT!
ARE TOO!
QUIT YOUR ROUGH-HOUSIN', BOYS!
AND DON'T PLAY WITH THAT BEAR RUG. IT COSTS MORE THAN YOUR LIVES!
AM NOT!
ARE TOO!
I'M GLAD YOU COULD COME CAMPIN' WITH ME IN MY STRATA-CRUISER 5000 DELUXE RV, LUANN, BUT WHY'D WE HAVE TO BRING THE MUNCHKINS?
I'M SORRY, BOB, BUT IT'S MY WEEKEND WITH MILHOUSE. I THOUGHT YOU TWO COULD DO A LITTLE BONDING.
WELL...UH-HUH ...YEAH, I GUESS I COULD TEACH HIM HOW TO EMPTY THE SEPTIC TANK.
I BROUGHT BART ALONG SO MILHOUSE WON'T CRY AT NIGHT.
MOM SAYS HE'S GOT DOWN-HOME HOSPITALITY, BUT I THINK HE'S A BIG JERK.
RV BOB IS SUCH A TOOL.
I HOPE HE DOESN'T TRY TO TEACH ME ANYTHING.

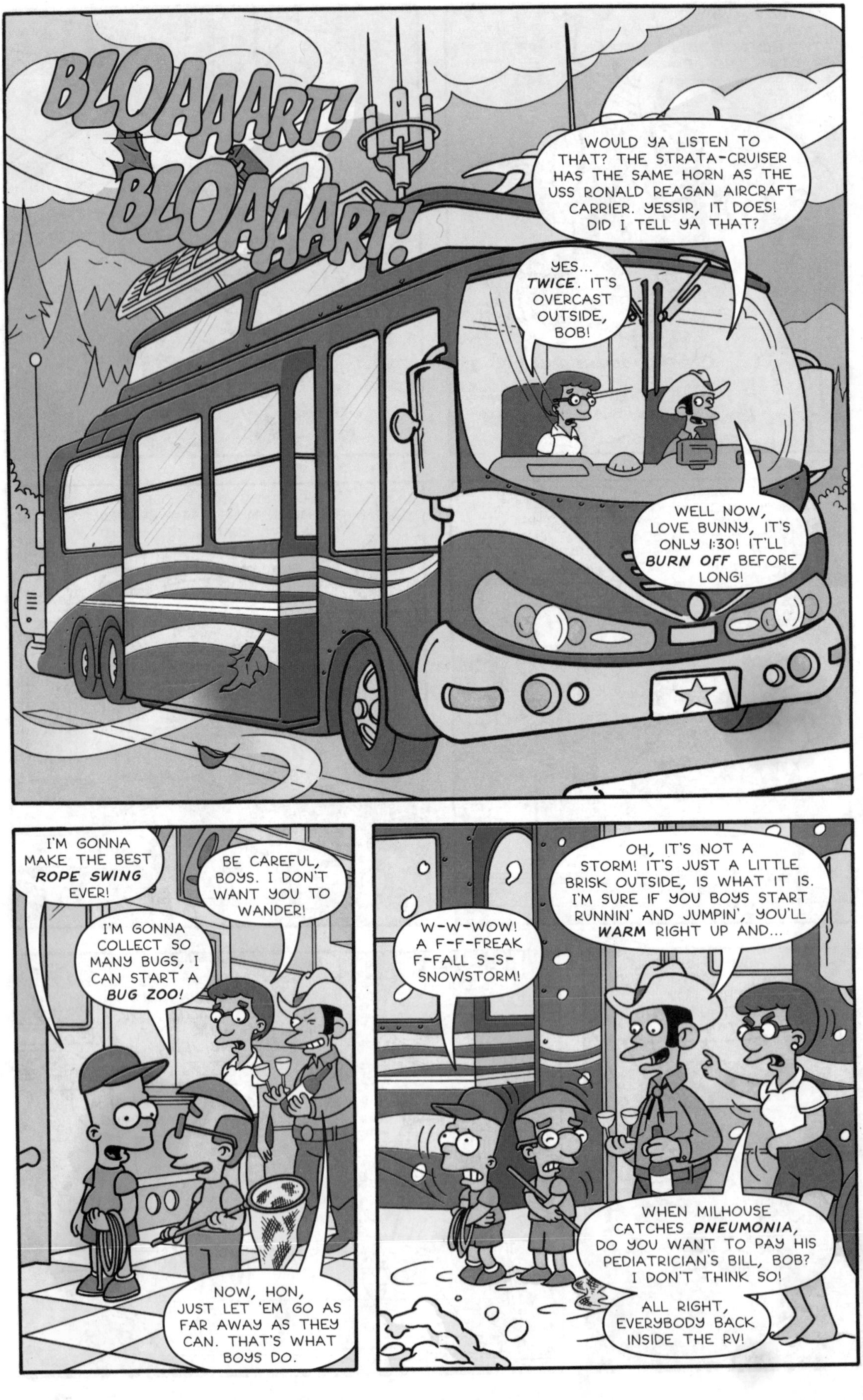
BLOAAART! BLOAAART!
WOULD YA LISTEN TO THAT? THE STRATA-CRUISER HAS THE SAME HORN AS THE USS RONALD REAGAN AIRCRAFT CARRIER. YESSIR, IT DOES! DID I TELL YA THAT?
YES... **TWICE**. IT'S OVERCAST OUTSIDE, BOB!
WELL NOW, LOVE BUNNY, IT'S ONLY 1:30! IT'LL **BURN OFF** BEFORE LONG!
I'M GONNA MAKE THE BEST **ROPE SWING** EVER!
I'M GONNA COLLECT SO MANY BUGS, I CAN START A **BUG ZOO**!
BE CAREFUL, BOYS. I DON'T WANT YOU TO WANDER!
NOW, HON, JUST LET 'EM GO AS FAR AWAY AS THEY CAN. THAT'S WHAT BOYS DO.
W-W-WOW! A F-F-FREAK F-FALL S-S-SNOWSTORM!
OH, IT'S NOT A STORM! IT'S JUST A LITTLE BRISK OUTSIDE, IS WHAT IT IS. I'M SURE IF YOU BOYS START RUNNIN' AND JUMPIN', YOU'LL **WARM** RIGHT UP AND...
WHEN MILHOUSE CATCHES **PNEUMONIA**, DO YOU WANT TO PAY HIS PEDIATRICIAN'S BILL, BOB? I DON'T THINK SO!
ALL RIGHT, EVERYBODY BACK INSIDE THE RV!

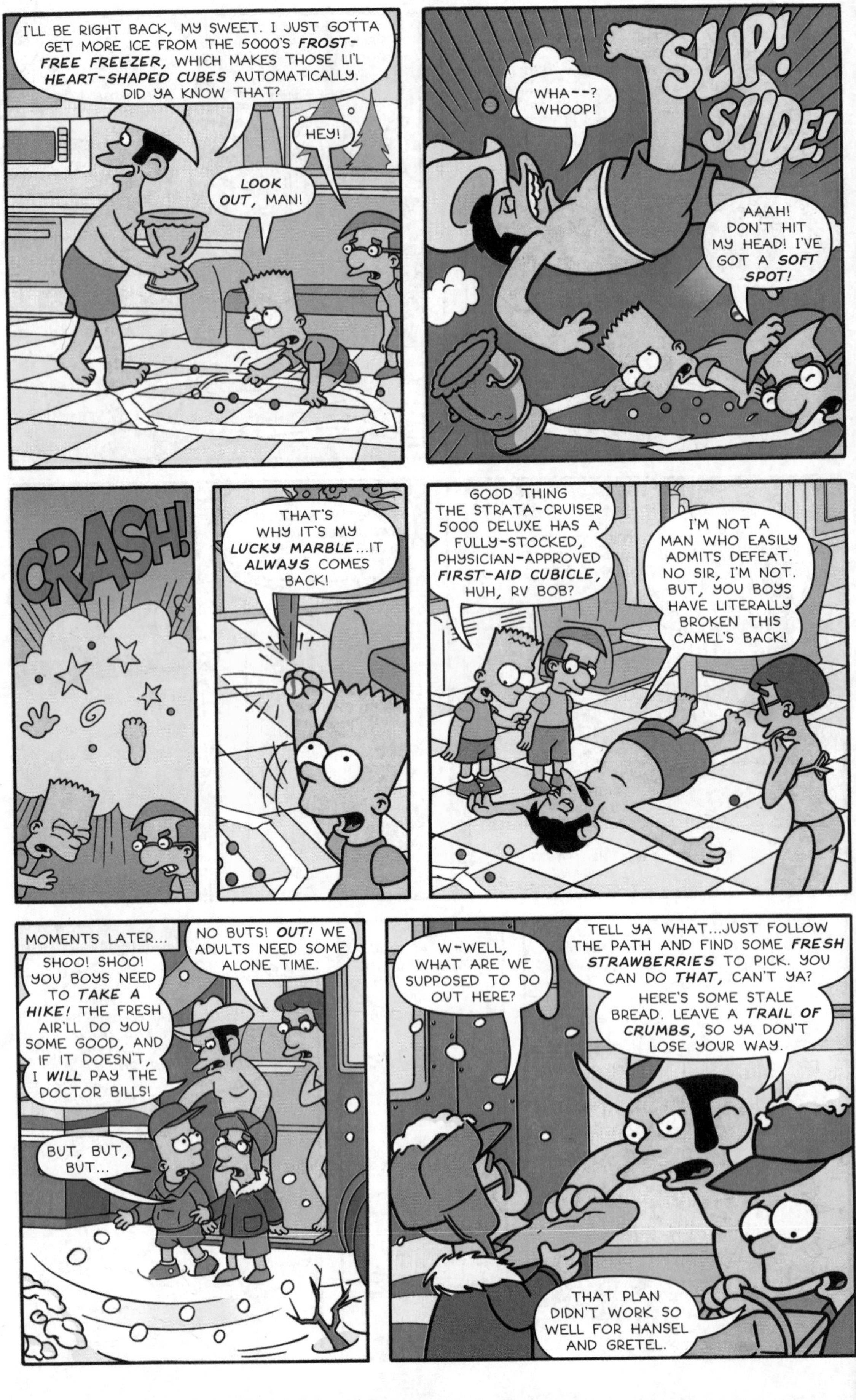
I'LL BE RIGHT BACK, MY SWEET. I JUST GOTTA GET MORE ICE FROM THE 5000'S FROST-FREE FREEZER, WHICH MAKES THOSE LI'L HEART-SHAPED CUBES AUTOMATICALLY. DID YA KNOW THAT?
HEY!
LOOK OUT, MAN!
WHA--? WHOOP!
SLIP! SLIDE!
AAAH! DON'T HIT MY HEAD! I'VE GOT A SOFT SPOT!
CRASH!
THAT'S WHY IT'S MY LUCKY MARBLE...IT ALWAYS COMES BACK!
GOOD THING THE STRATA-CRUISER 5000 DELUXE HAS A FULLY-STOCKED, PHYSICIAN-APPROVED FIRST-AID CUBICLE, HUH, RV BOB?
I'M NOT A MAN WHO EASILY ADMITS DEFEAT. NO SIR, I'M NOT. BUT, YOU BOYS HAVE LITERALLY BROKEN THIS CAMEL'S BACK!
MOMENTS LATER...
SHOO! SHOO! YOU BOYS NEED TO TAKE A HIKE! THE FRESH AIR'LL DO YOU SOME GOOD, AND IF IT DOESN'T, I WILL PAY THE DOCTOR BILLS!
NO BUTS! OUT! WE ADULTS NEED SOME ALONE TIME.
BUT, BUT, BUT...
W-WELL, WHAT ARE WE SUPPOSED TO DO OUT HERE?
TELL YA WHAT...JUST FOLLOW THE PATH AND FIND SOME FRESH STRAWBERRIES TO PICK. YOU CAN DO THAT, CAN'T YA?
HERE'S SOME STALE BREAD. LEAVE A TRAIL OF CRUMBS, SO YA DON'T LOSE YOUR WAY.
THAT PLAN DIDN'T WORK SO WELL FOR HANSEL AND GRETEL.

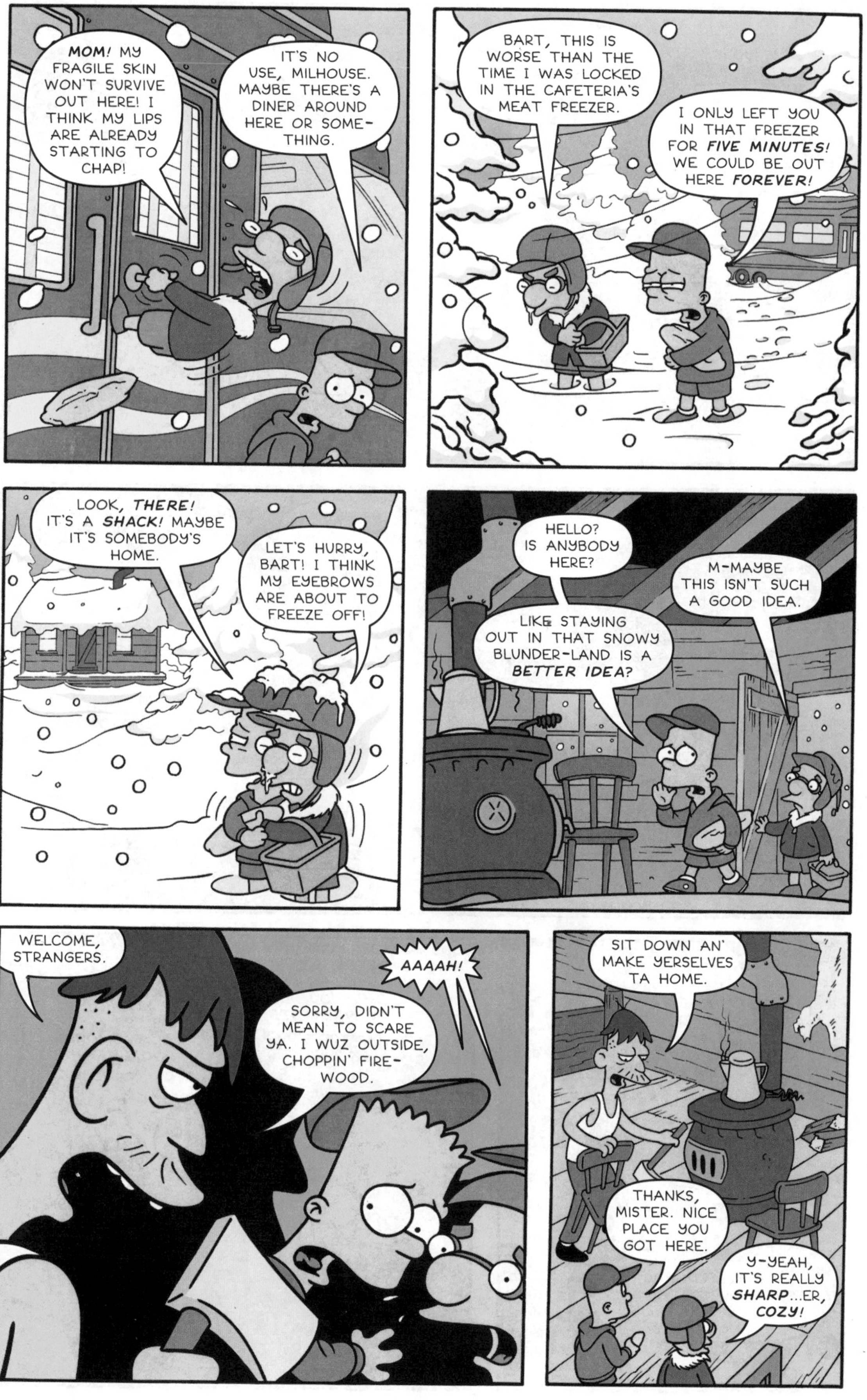
MOM! MY FRAGILE SKIN WON'T SURVIVE OUT HERE! I THINK MY LIPS ARE ALREADY STARTING TO CHAP!
IT'S NO USE, MILHOUSE. MAYBE THERE'S A DINER AROUND HERE OR SOME-THING.
BART, THIS IS WORSE THAN THE TIME I WAS LOCKED IN THE CAFETERIA'S MEAT FREEZER.
I ONLY LEFT YOU IN THAT FREEZER FOR FIVE MINUTES! WE COULD BE OUT HERE FOREVER!
LOOK, THERE! IT'S A SHACK! MAYBE IT'S SOMEBODY'S HOME.
LET'S HURRY, BART! I THINK MY EYEBROWS ARE ABOUT TO FREEZE OFF!
HELLO? IS ANYBODY HERE?
M-MAYBE THIS ISN'T SUCH A GOOD IDEA.
LIKE STAYING OUT IN THAT SNOWY BLUNDER-LAND IS A BETTER IDEA?
WELCOME, STRANGERS.
AAAAH!
SORRY, DIDN'T MEAN TO SCARE YA. I WUZ OUTSIDE, CHOPPIN' FIRE-WOOD.
SIT DOWN AN' MAKE YERSELVES TA HOME.
THANKS, MISTER. NICE PLACE YOU GOT HERE.
Y-YEAH, IT'S REALLY SHARP...ER, COZY!

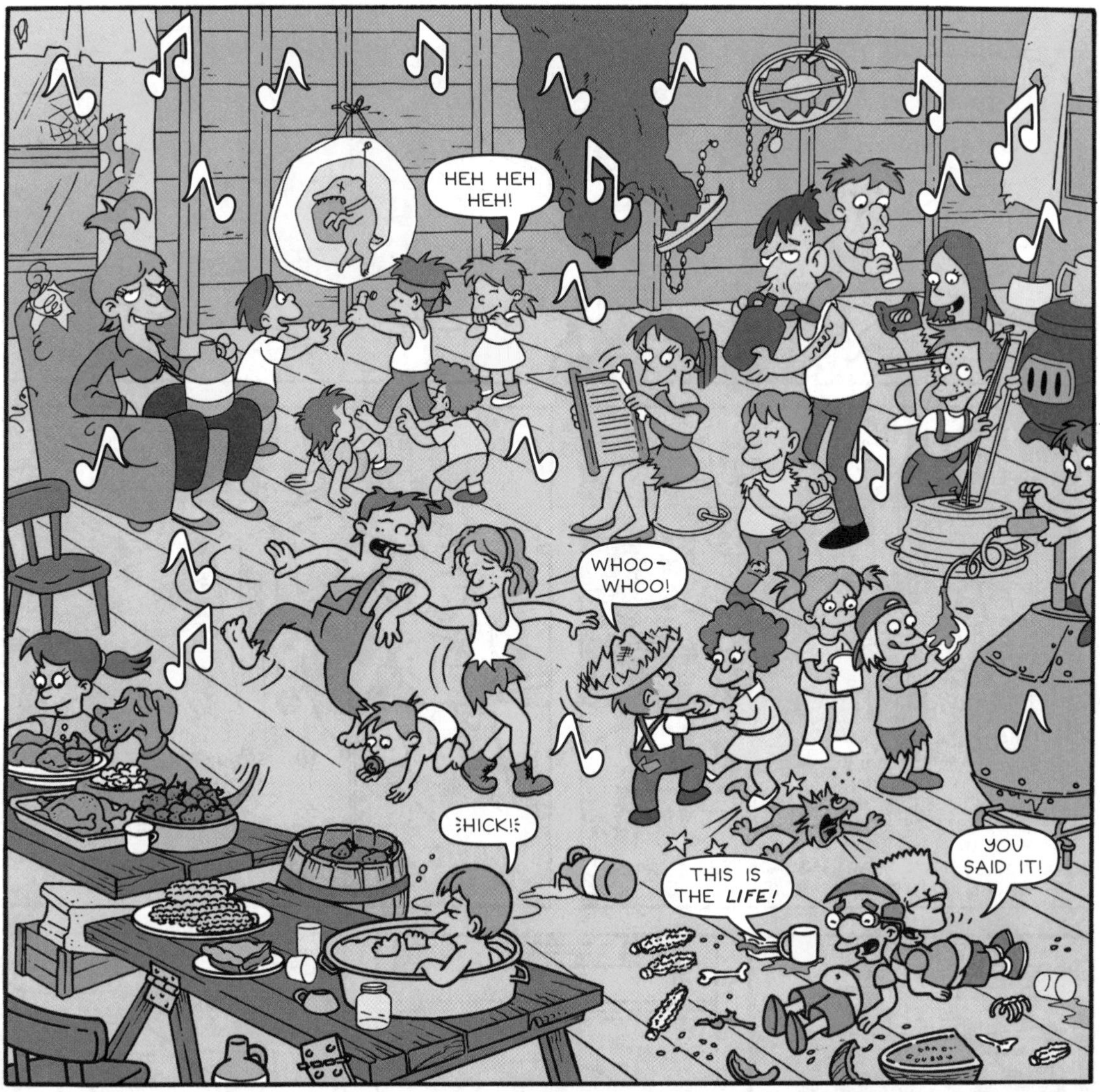
HEH HEH HEH!
WHOO-WHOO!
HICK!
THIS IS THE *LIFE!*
YOU SAID IT!

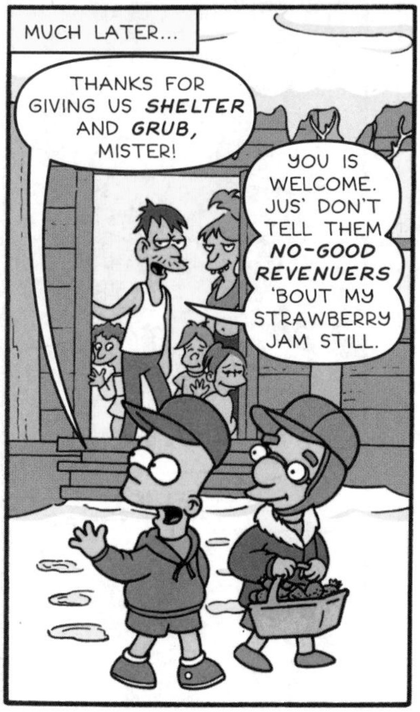
MUCH LATER...
THANKS FOR GIVING US *SHELTER* AND *GRUB,* MISTER!
YOU IS WELCOME. JUS' DON'T TELL THEM ***NO-GOOD REVENUERS*** 'BOUT MY STRAWBERRY JAM STILL.

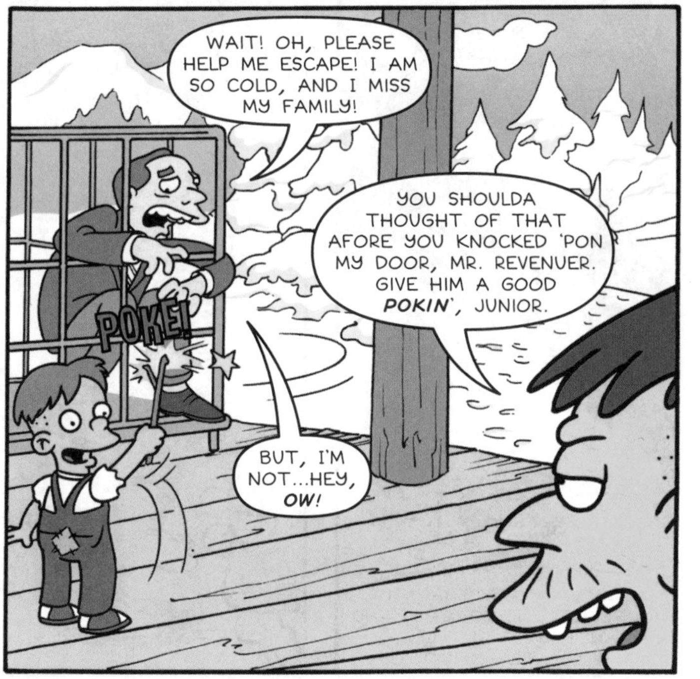
WAIT! OH, PLEASE HELP ME ESCAPE! I AM SO COLD, AND I MISS MY FAMILY!
YOU SHOULDA THOUGHT OF THAT AFORE YOU KNOCKED 'PON MY DOOR, MR. REVENUER. GIVE HIM A GOOD ***POKIN'***, JUNIOR.
POKE!
BUT, I'M NOT...HEY, ***OW!***

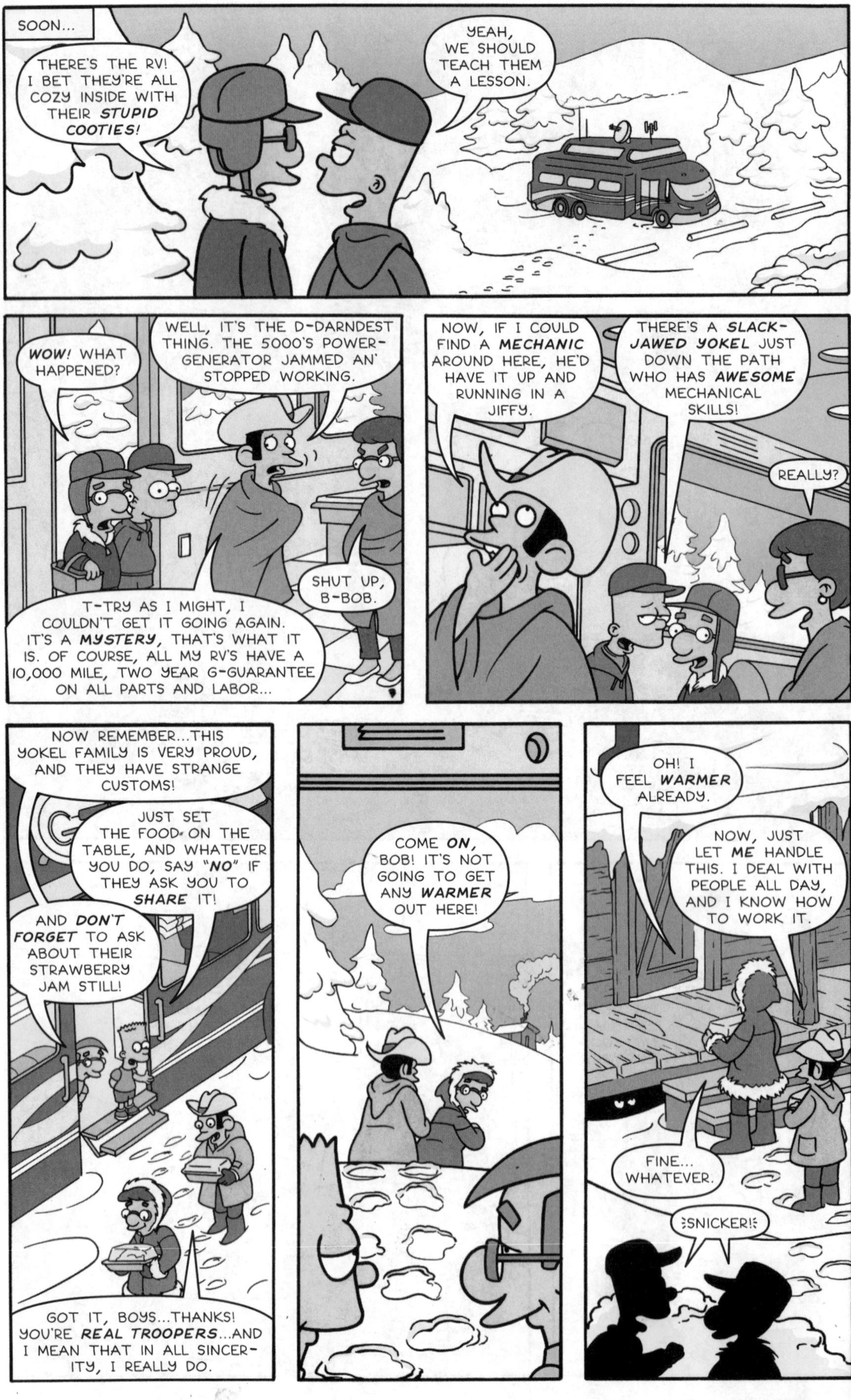
SOON...
THERE'S THE RV! I BET THEY'RE ALL COZY INSIDE WITH THEIR STUPID COOTIES!
YEAH, WE SHOULD TEACH THEM A LESSON.
WOW! WHAT HAPPENED?
WELL, IT'S THE D-DARNDEST THING. THE 5000'S POWER-GENERATOR JAMMED AN' STOPPED WORKING.
SHUT UP, B-BOB.
T-TRY AS I MIGHT, I COULDN'T GET IT GOING AGAIN. IT'S A MYSTERY, THAT'S WHAT IT IS. OF COURSE, ALL MY RV'S HAVE A 10,000 MILE, TWO YEAR G-GUARANTEE ON ALL PARTS AND LABOR...
NOW, IF I COULD FIND A MECHANIC AROUND HERE, HE'D HAVE IT UP AND RUNNING IN A JIFFY.
THERE'S A SLACK-JAWED YOKEL JUST DOWN THE PATH WHO HAS AWESOME MECHANICAL SKILLS!
REALLY?
NOW REMEMBER...THIS YOKEL FAMILY IS VERY PROUD, AND THEY HAVE STRANGE CUSTOMS!
JUST SET THE FOOD ON THE TABLE, AND WHATEVER YOU DO, SAY "NO" IF THEY ASK YOU TO SHARE IT!
AND DON'T FORGET TO ASK ABOUT THEIR STRAWBERRY JAM STILL!
GOT IT, BOYS...THANKS! YOU'RE REAL TROOPERS...AND I MEAN THAT IN ALL SINCERITY, I REALLY DO.
COME ON, BOB! IT'S NOT GOING TO GET ANY WARMER OUT HERE!
OH! I FEEL WARMER ALREADY.
NOW, JUST LET ME HANDLE THIS. I DEAL WITH PEOPLE ALL DAY, AND I KNOW HOW TO WORK IT.
FINE... WHATEVER.
SNICKER!

LATER, BACK AT THE RV...

THE END

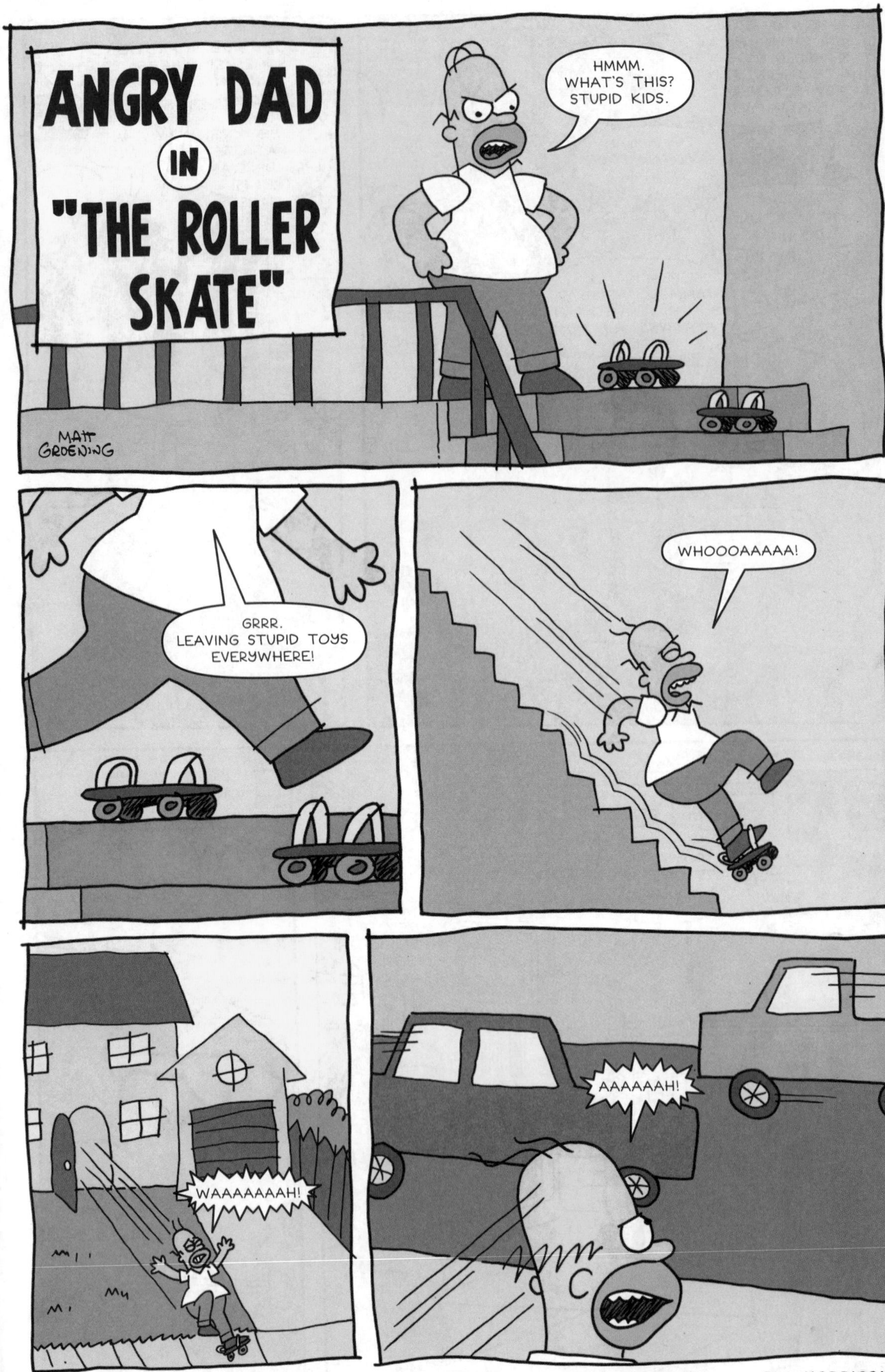
ANGRY DAD
IN
"THE ROLLER SKATE"
MATT GROENING
HMMM. WHAT'S THIS? STUPID KIDS.
GRRR. LEAVING STUPID TOYS EVERYWHERE!
WHOOOAAAAA!
WAAAAAAAAH!
AAAAAAH!

TONY DIGEROLAMO SCRIPT · ***JASON HO*** PENCILS & INKS · ***TERRY DELEGEANE*** COLORS · ***KAREN BATES*** LETTERS · ***BILL MORRISON*** EDITOR

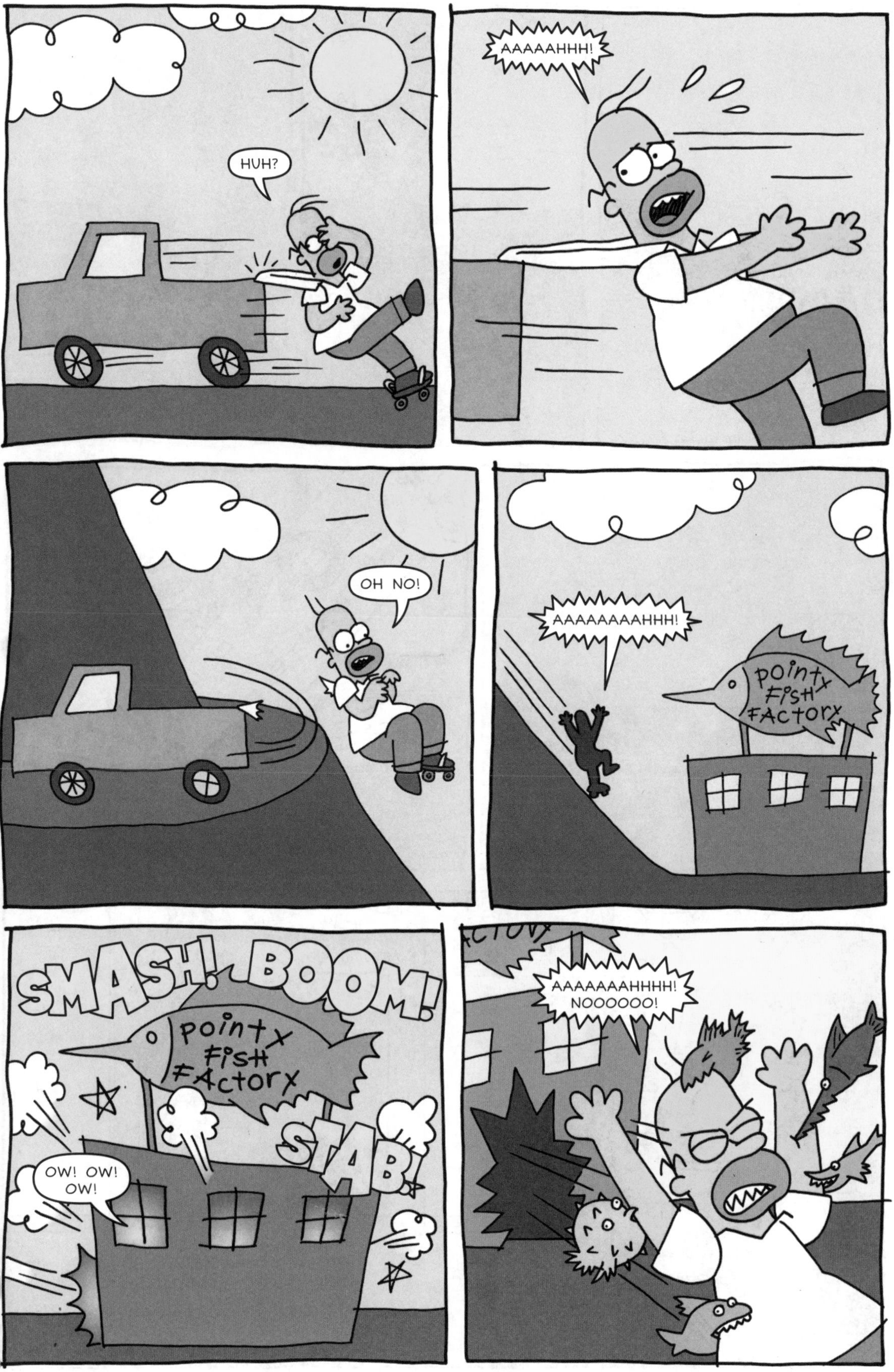
HUH?
AAAAAHHH!
OH NO!
AAAAAAAAHHH!
pointy Fish Factory
SMASH! BOOM!
pointy Fish Factory
STAB!
OW! OW! OW!
AAAAAAAHHHH! NOOOOOO!

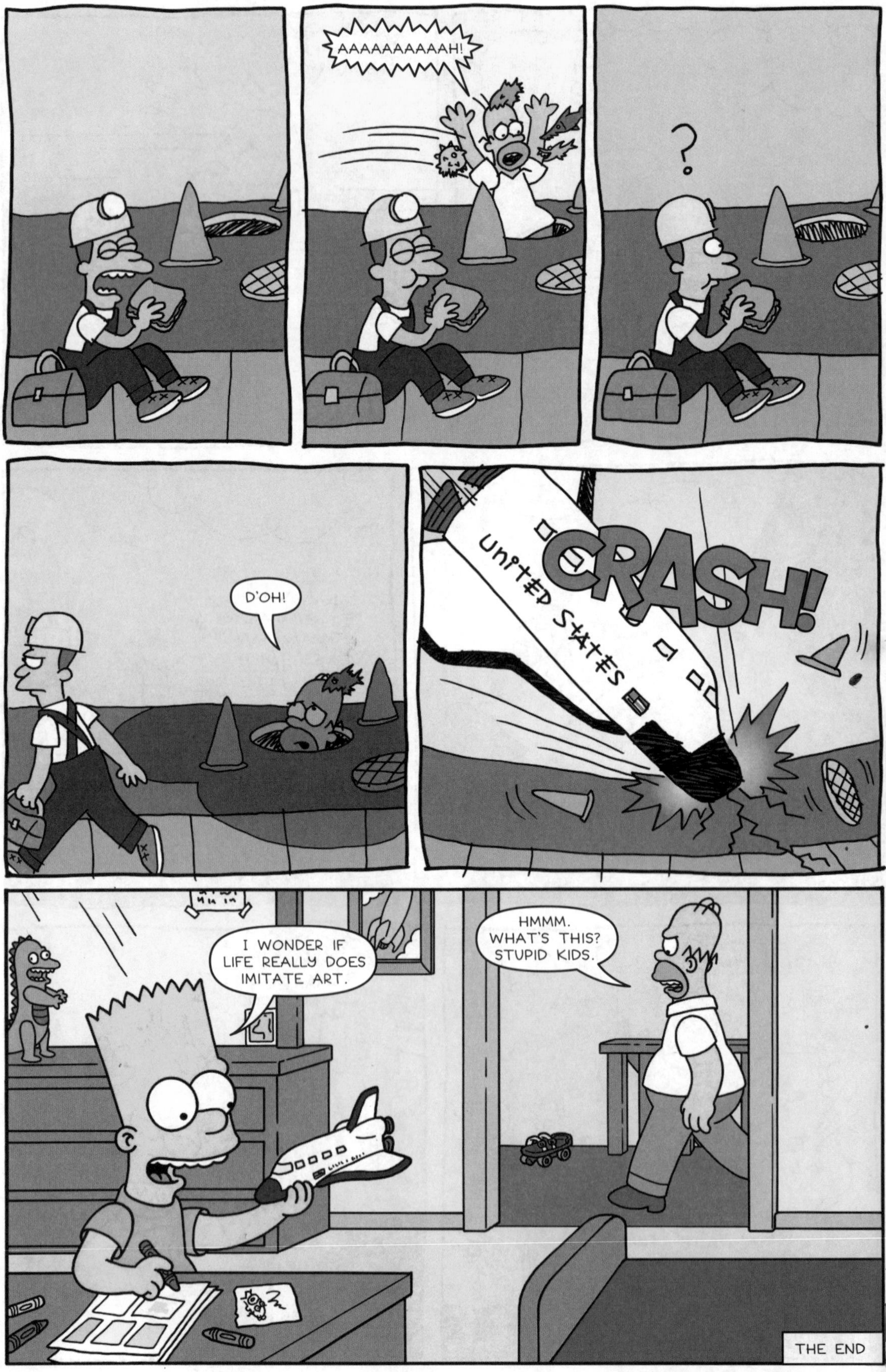
AAAAAAAAAAAH!
?
D'OH!
UNITED STATES
CRASH!
I WONDER IF LIFE REALLY DOES IMITATE ART.
HMMM. WHAT'S THIS? STUPID KIDS.
THE END

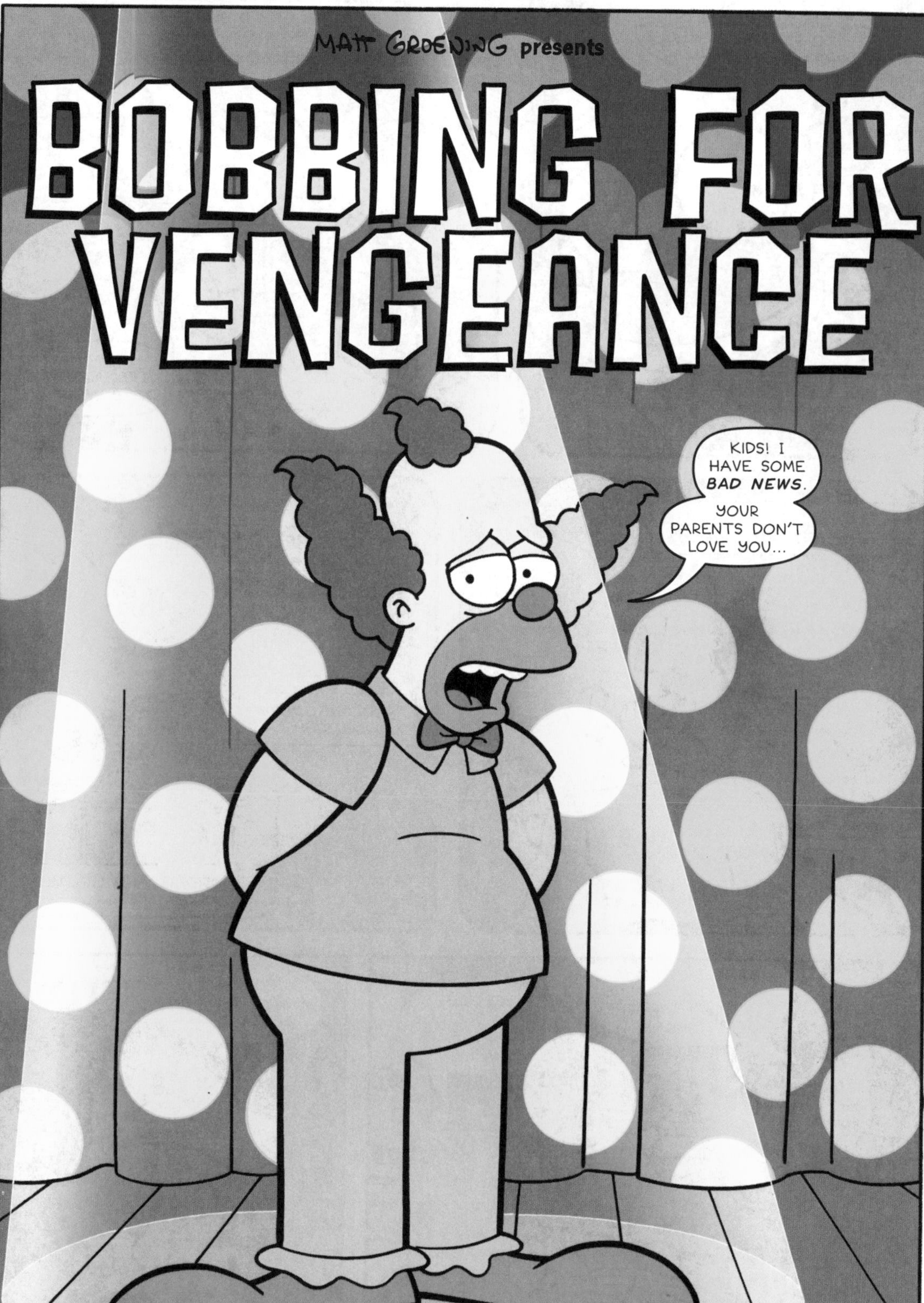
MATT GROENING presents
BOBBING FOR VENGEANCE
KIDS! I HAVE SOME BAD NEWS.
YOUR PARENTS DON'T LOVE YOU...

IAN BOOTHBY SCRIPT PHIL ORTIZ PENCILS MIKE DECARLO INKS ART VILLANUEVA COLORS KAREN BATES LETTERS BILL MORRISON EDITOR

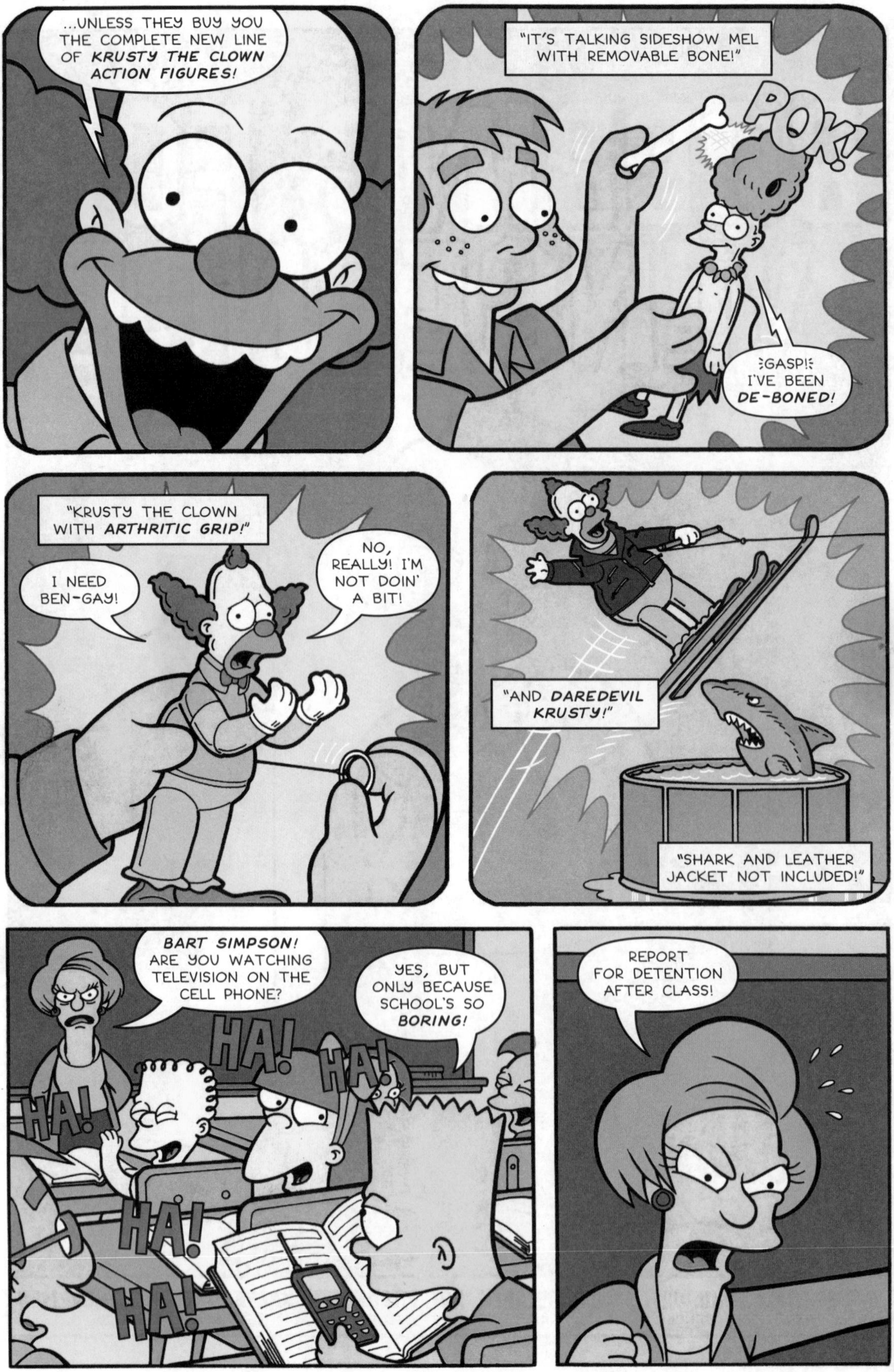
...UNLESS THEY BUY YOU THE COMPLETE NEW LINE OF KRUSTY THE CLOWN ACTION FIGURES!
"IT'S TALKING SIDESHOW MEL WITH REMOVABLE BONE!"
POK!
GASP! I'VE BEEN DE-BONED!
"KRUSTY THE CLOWN WITH ARTHRITIC GRIP!"
I NEED BEN-GAY!
NO, REALLY! I'M NOT DOIN' A BIT!
"AND DAREDEVIL KRUSTY!"
"SHARK AND LEATHER JACKET NOT INCLUDED!"
BART SIMPSON! ARE YOU WATCHING TELEVISION ON THE CELL PHONE?
YES, BUT ONLY BECAUSE SCHOOL'S SO BORING!
HA! HA! HA! HA! HA!
REPORT FOR DETENTION AFTER CLASS!

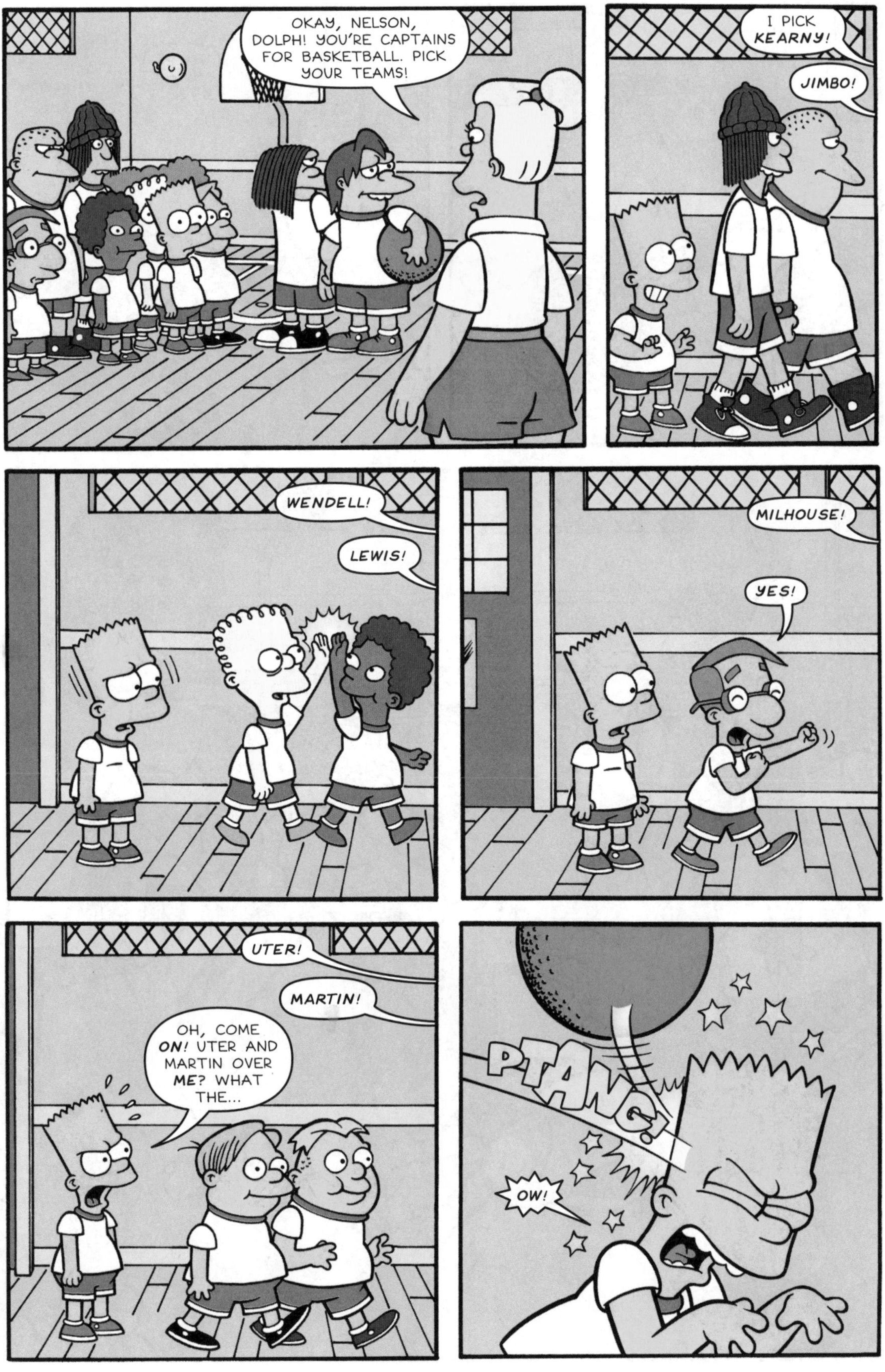

OKAY, NELSON, DOLPH! YOU'RE CAPTAINS FOR BASKETBALL. PICK YOUR TEAMS!
I PICK KEARNY!
JIMBO!
WENDELL!
LEWIS!
MILHOUSE!
YES!
UTER!
MARTIN!
OH, COME ON! UTER AND MARTIN OVER ME? WHAT THE...
PTANG!
OW!

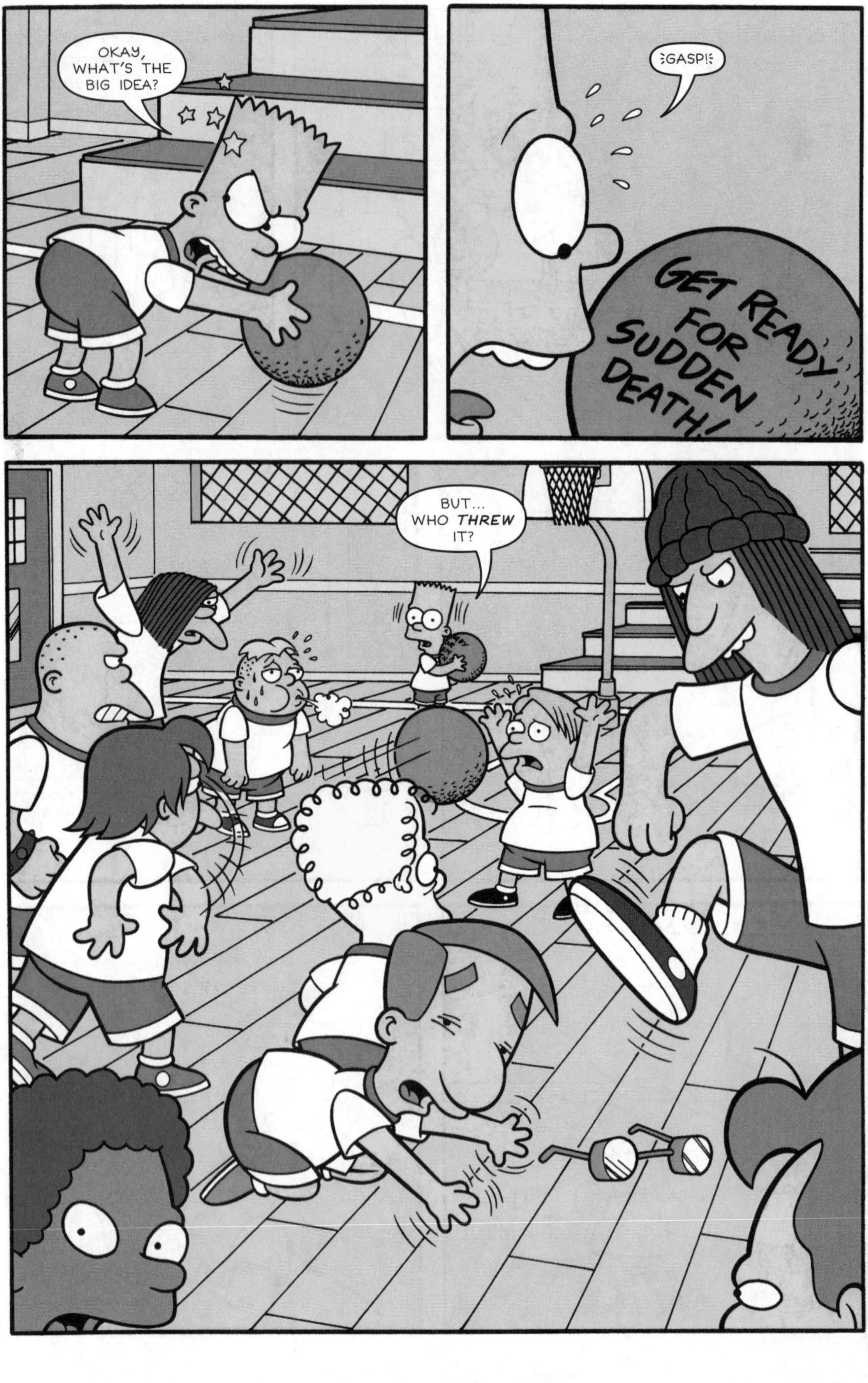
OKAY, WHAT'S THE BIG IDEA?
GASP!
GET READY FOR SUDDEN DEATH!
BUT... WHO THREW IT?

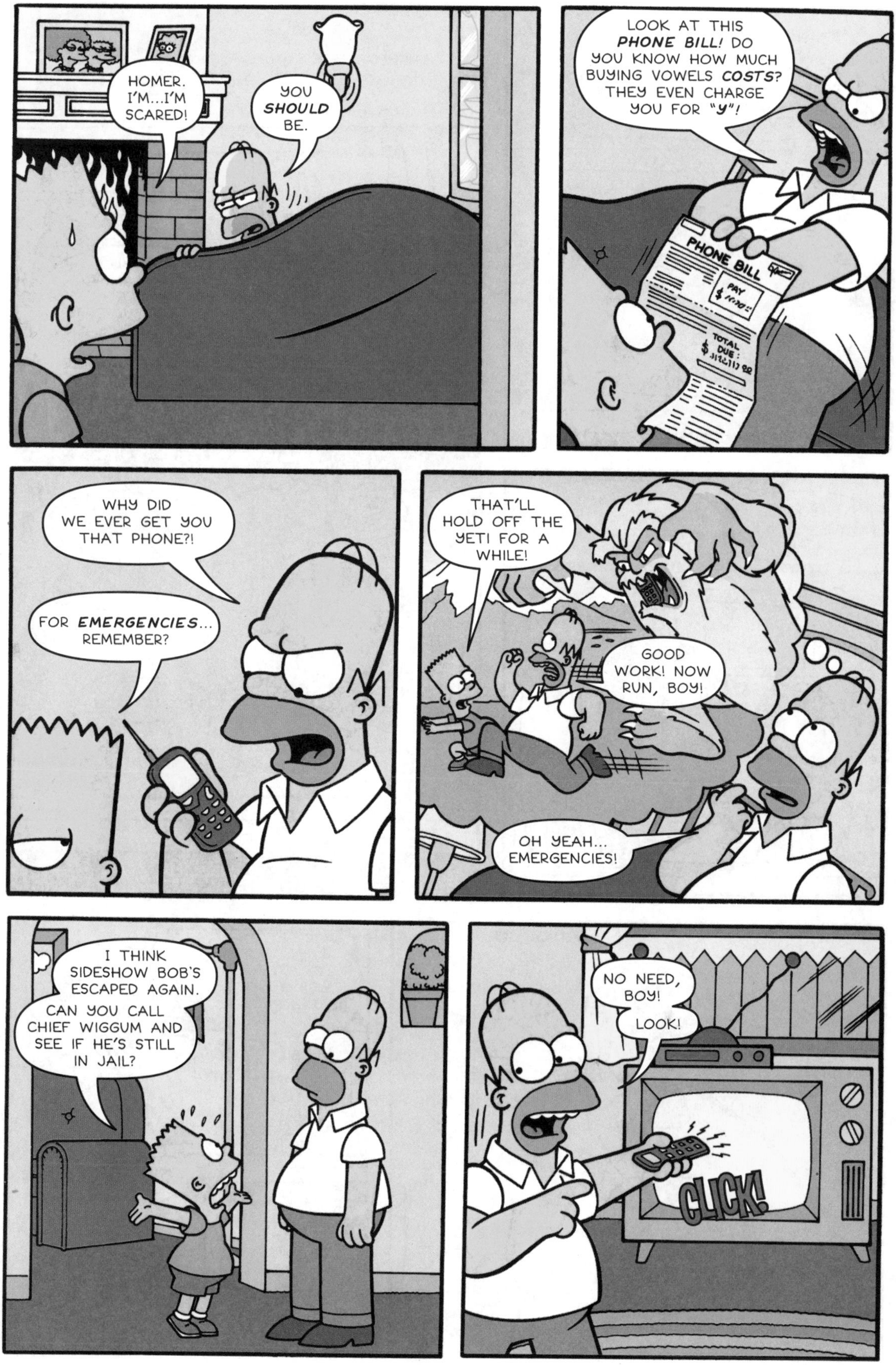

HOMER. I'M...I'M SCARED!
YOU *SHOULD* BE.
LOOK AT THIS *PHONE BILL!* DO YOU KNOW HOW MUCH BUYING VOWELS *COSTS?* THEY EVEN CHARGE YOU FOR "*Y*"!
PHONE BILL
PAY
TOTAL DUE:
WHY DID WE EVER GET YOU THAT PHONE?!
FOR *EMERGENCIES*... REMEMBER?
THAT'LL HOLD OFF THE YETI FOR A WHILE!
GOOD WORK! NOW RUN, BOY!
OH YEAH... EMERGENCIES!
I THINK SIDESHOW BOB'S ESCAPED AGAIN.
CAN YOU CALL CHIEF WIGGUM AND SEE IF HE'S STILL IN JAIL?
NO NEED, BOY!
LOOK!
CLICK!

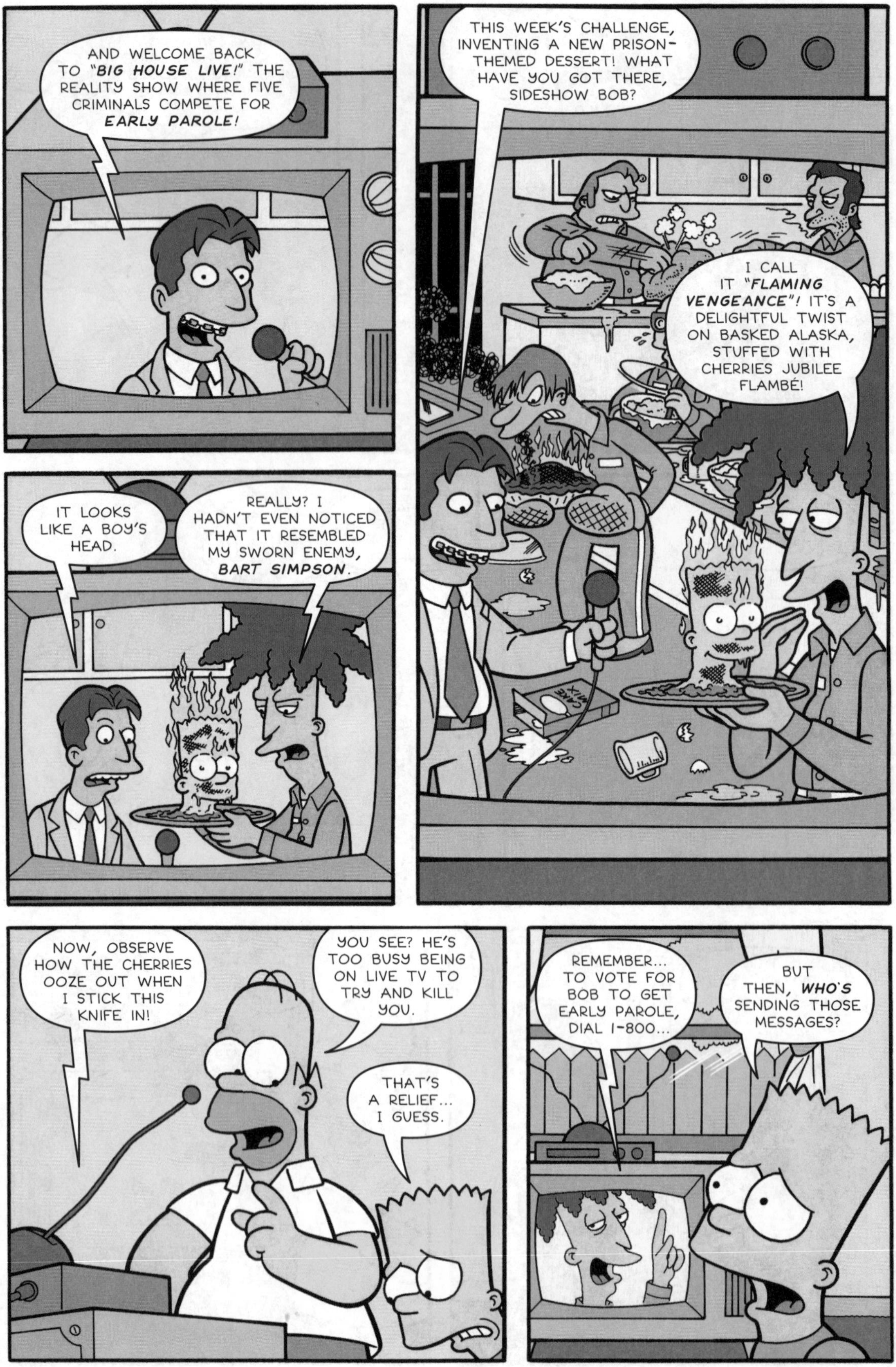
AND WELCOME BACK TO "BIG HOUSE LIVE!" THE REALITY SHOW WHERE FIVE CRIMINALS COMPETE FOR EARLY PAROLE!
THIS WEEK'S CHALLENGE, INVENTING A NEW PRISON-THEMED DESSERT! WHAT HAVE YOU GOT THERE, SIDESHOW BOB?
I CALL IT "FLAMING VENGEANCE"! IT'S A DELIGHTFUL TWIST ON BASKED ALASKA, STUFFED WITH CHERRIES JUBILEE FLAMBÉ!
IT LOOKS LIKE A BOY'S HEAD.
REALLY? I HADN'T EVEN NOTICED THAT IT RESEMBLED MY SWORN ENEMY, BART SIMPSON.
NOW, OBSERVE HOW THE CHERRIES OOZE OUT WHEN I STICK THIS KNIFE IN!
YOU SEE? HE'S TOO BUSY BEING ON LIVE TV TO TRY AND KILL YOU.
THAT'S A RELIEF... I GUESS.
REMEMBER... TO VOTE FOR BOB TO GET EARLY PAROLE, DIAL 1-800...
BUT THEN, WHO'S SENDING THOSE MESSAGES?

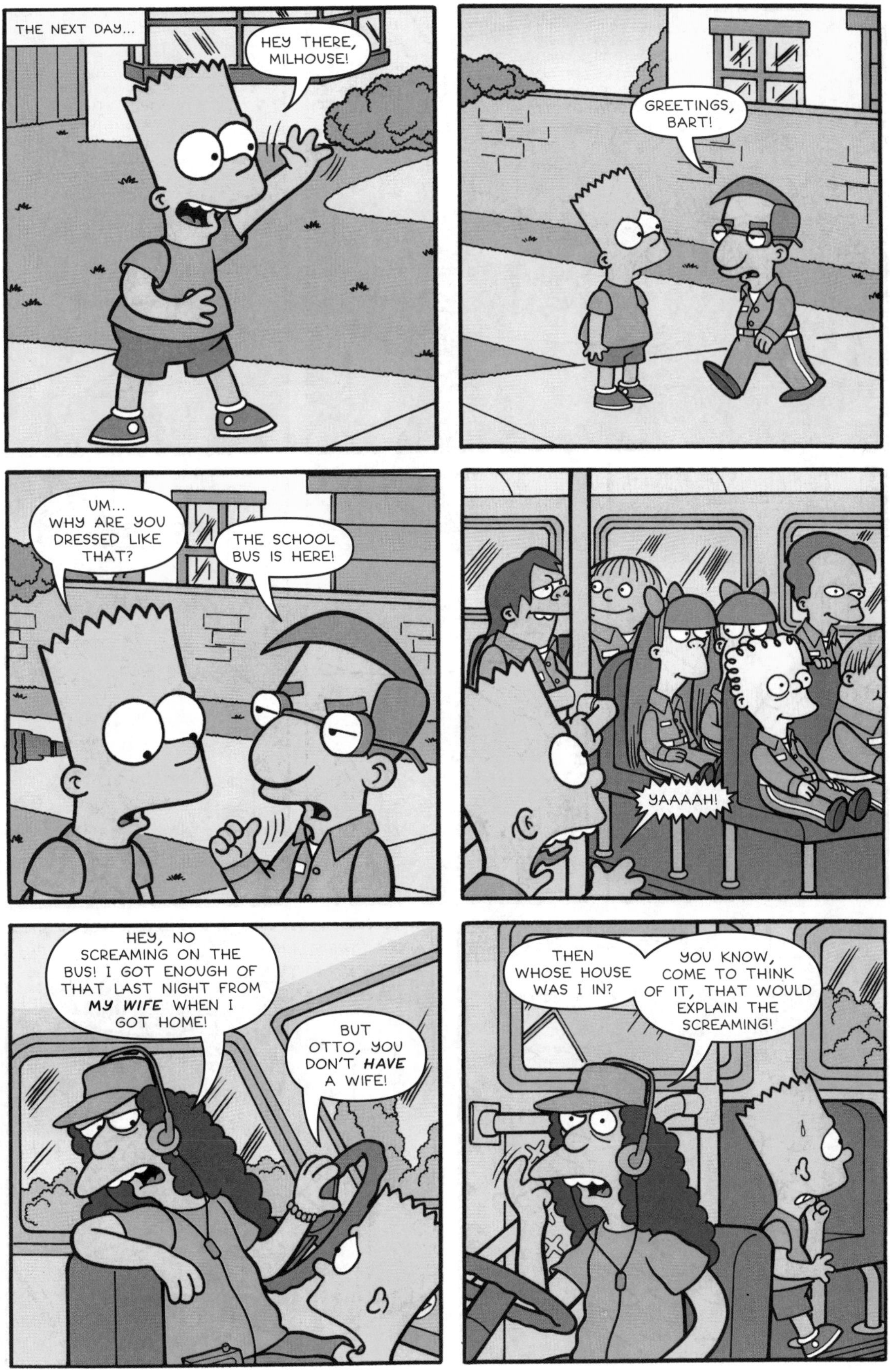
THE NEXT DAY...
HEY THERE, MILHOUSE!
GREETINGS, BART!
UM... WHY ARE YOU DRESSED LIKE THAT?
THE SCHOOL BUS IS HERE!
YAAAAH!
HEY, NO SCREAMING ON THE BUS! I GOT ENOUGH OF THAT LAST NIGHT FROM MY WIFE WHEN I GOT HOME!
BUT OTTO, YOU DON'T HAVE A WIFE!
THEN WHOSE HOUSE WAS I IN?
YOU KNOW, COME TO THINK OF IT, THAT WOULD EXPLAIN THE SCREAMING!

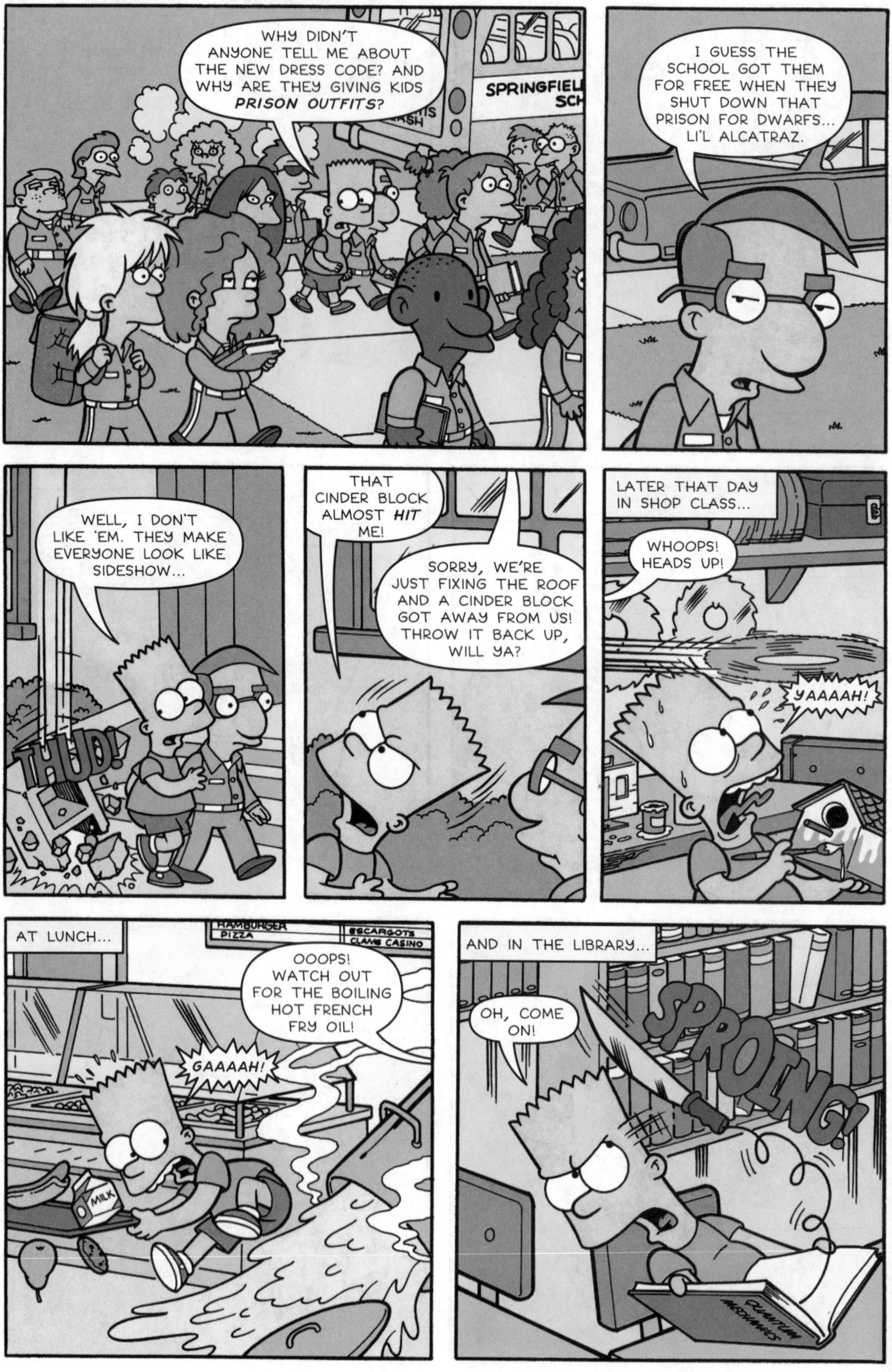
WHY DIDN'T ANYONE TELL ME ABOUT THE NEW DRESS CODE? AND WHY ARE THEY GIVING KIDS *PRISON OUTFITS*?
SPRINGFIELD SCH
I GUESS THE SCHOOL GOT THEM FOR FREE WHEN THEY SHUT DOWN THAT PRISON FOR DWARFS... LI'L ALCATRAZ.
WELL, I DON'T LIKE 'EM. THEY MAKE EVERYONE LOOK LIKE SIDESHOW...
THUD!
THAT CINDER BLOCK ALMOST *HIT* ME!
SORRY, WE'RE JUST FIXING THE ROOF AND A CINDER BLOCK GOT AWAY FROM US! THROW IT BACK UP, WILL YA?
LATER THAT DAY IN SHOP CLASS...
WHOOPS! HEADS UP!
YAAAAH!
AT LUNCH...
HAMBURGER
PIZZA
ESCARGOTS
CLAMS CASINO
OOOPS! WATCH OUT FOR THE BOILING HOT FRENCH FRY OIL!
GAAAAH!
MILK
AND IN THE LIBRARY...
OH, COME ON!
SPROING!
QUANTUM MECHANICS

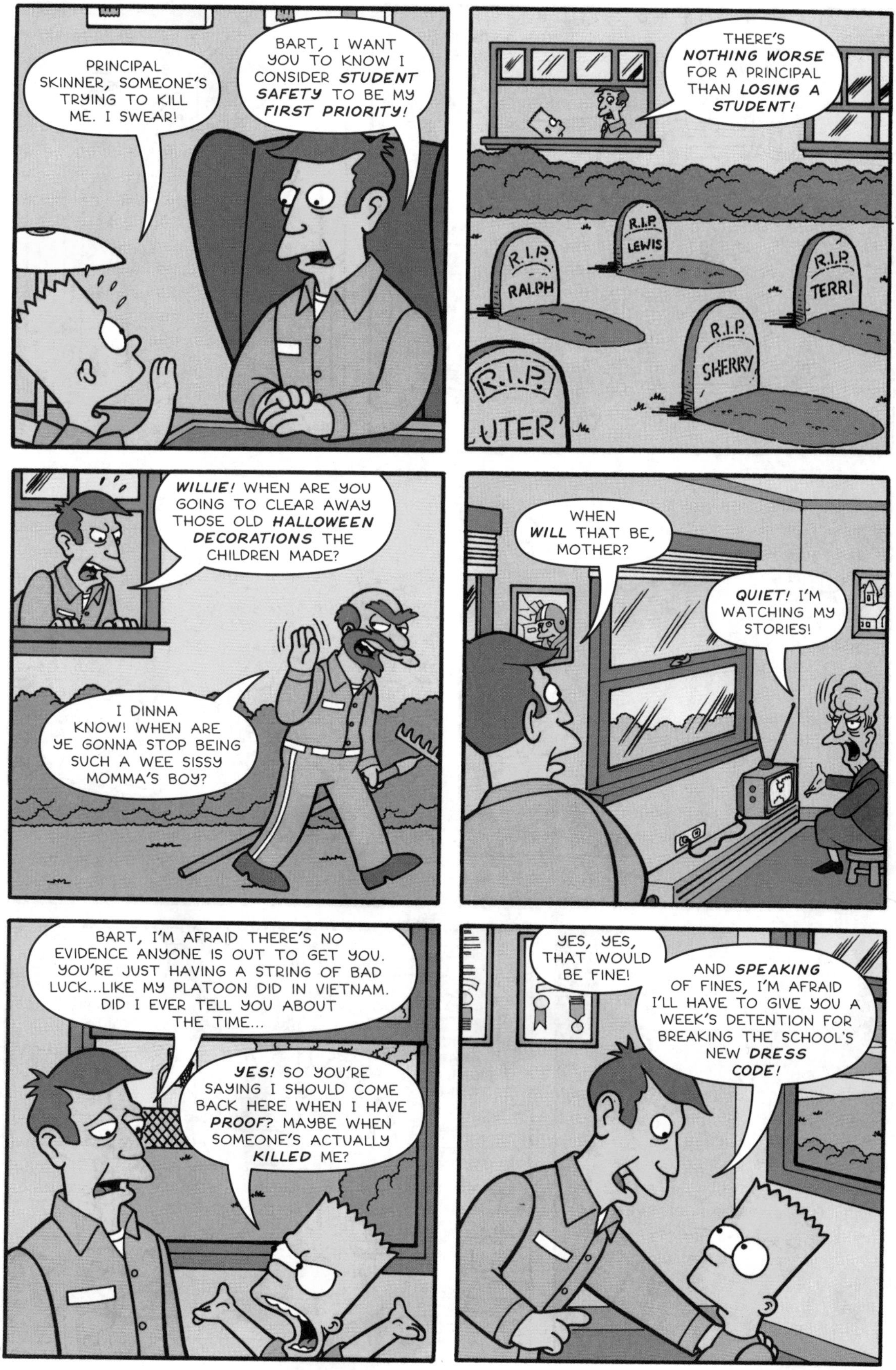
PRINCIPAL SKINNER, SOMEONE'S TRYING TO KILL ME. I SWEAR!
BART, I WANT YOU TO KNOW I CONSIDER STUDENT SAFETY TO BE MY FIRST PRIORITY!
THERE'S NOTHING WORSE FOR A PRINCIPAL THAN LOSING A STUDENT!
R.I.P. LEWIS
R.I.P. RALPH
R.I.P. TERRI
R.I.P. SHERRY
R.I.P.
UTER
WILLIE! WHEN ARE YOU GOING TO CLEAR AWAY THOSE OLD HALLOWEEN DECORATIONS THE CHILDREN MADE?
I DINNA KNOW! WHEN ARE YE GONNA STOP BEING SUCH A WEE SISSY MOMMA'S BOY?
WHEN WILL THAT BE, MOTHER?
QUIET! I'M WATCHING MY STORIES!
BART, I'M AFRAID THERE'S NO EVIDENCE ANYONE IS OUT TO GET YOU. YOU'RE JUST HAVING A STRING OF BAD LUCK...LIKE MY PLATOON DID IN VIETNAM. DID I EVER TELL YOU ABOUT THE TIME...
YES! SO YOU'RE SAYING I SHOULD COME BACK HERE WHEN I HAVE PROOF? MAYBE WHEN SOMEONE'S ACTUALLY KILLED ME?
YES, YES, THAT WOULD BE FINE!
AND SPEAKING OF FINES, I'M AFRAID I'LL HAVE TO GIVE YOU A WEEK'S DETENTION FOR BREAKING THE SCHOOL'S NEW DRESS CODE!

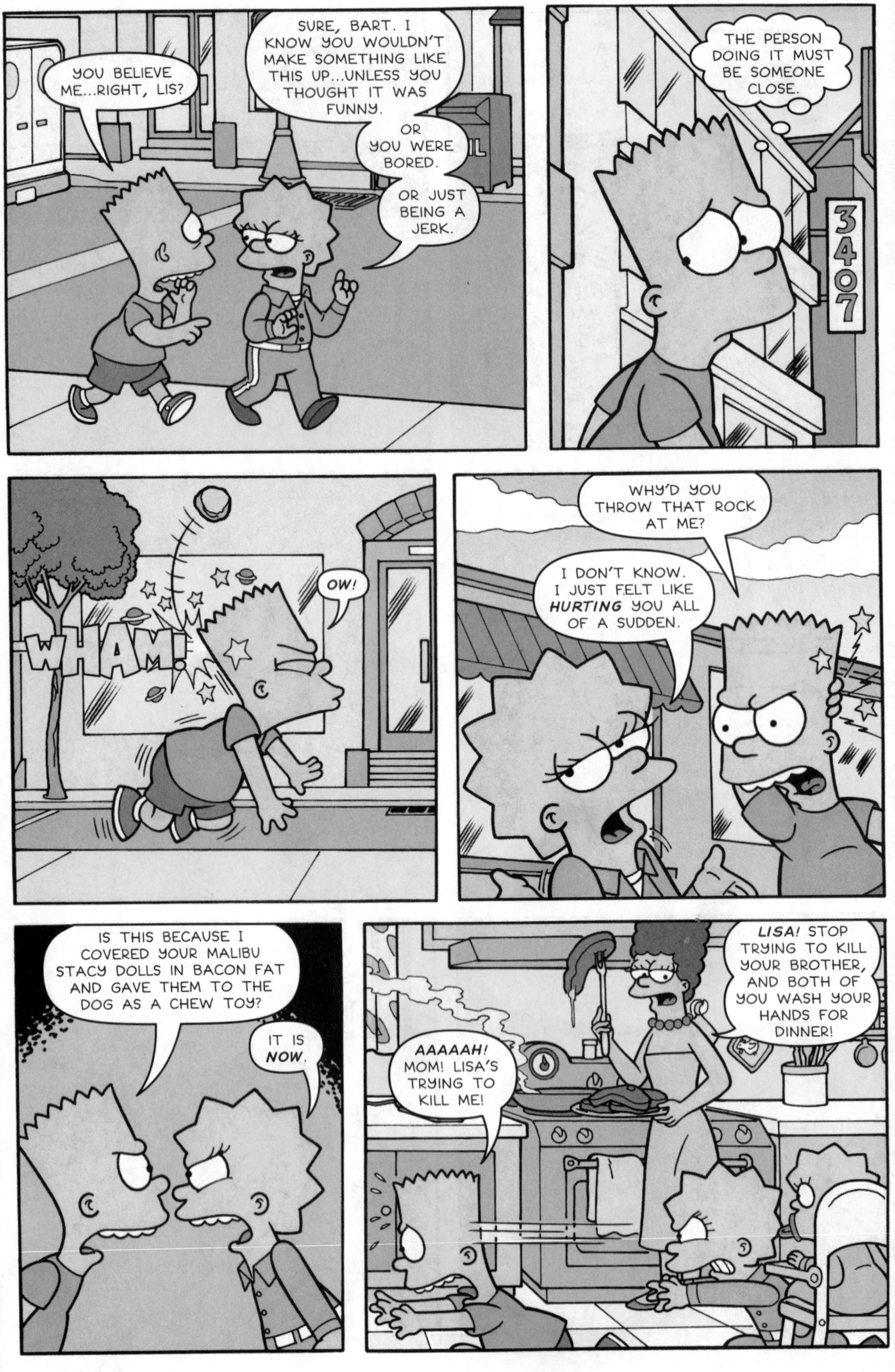
YOU BELIEVE ME...RIGHT, LIS?
SURE, BART. I KNOW YOU WOULDN'T MAKE SOMETHING LIKE THIS UP...UNLESS YOU THOUGHT IT WAS FUNNY.
OR YOU WERE BORED.
OR JUST BEING A JERK.
THE PERSON DOING IT MUST BE SOMEONE CLOSE.
3407
WHAM!
OW!
WHY'D YOU THROW THAT ROCK AT ME?
I DON'T KNOW. I JUST FELT LIKE *HURTING* YOU ALL OF A SUDDEN.
IS THIS BECAUSE I COVERED YOUR MALIBU STACY DOLLS IN BACON FAT AND GAVE THEM TO THE DOG AS A CHEW TOY?
IT IS *NOW*.
AAAAAH! MOM! LISA'S TRYING TO KILL ME!
LISA! STOP TRYING TO KILL YOUR BROTHER, AND BOTH OF YOU WASH YOUR HANDS FOR DINNER!

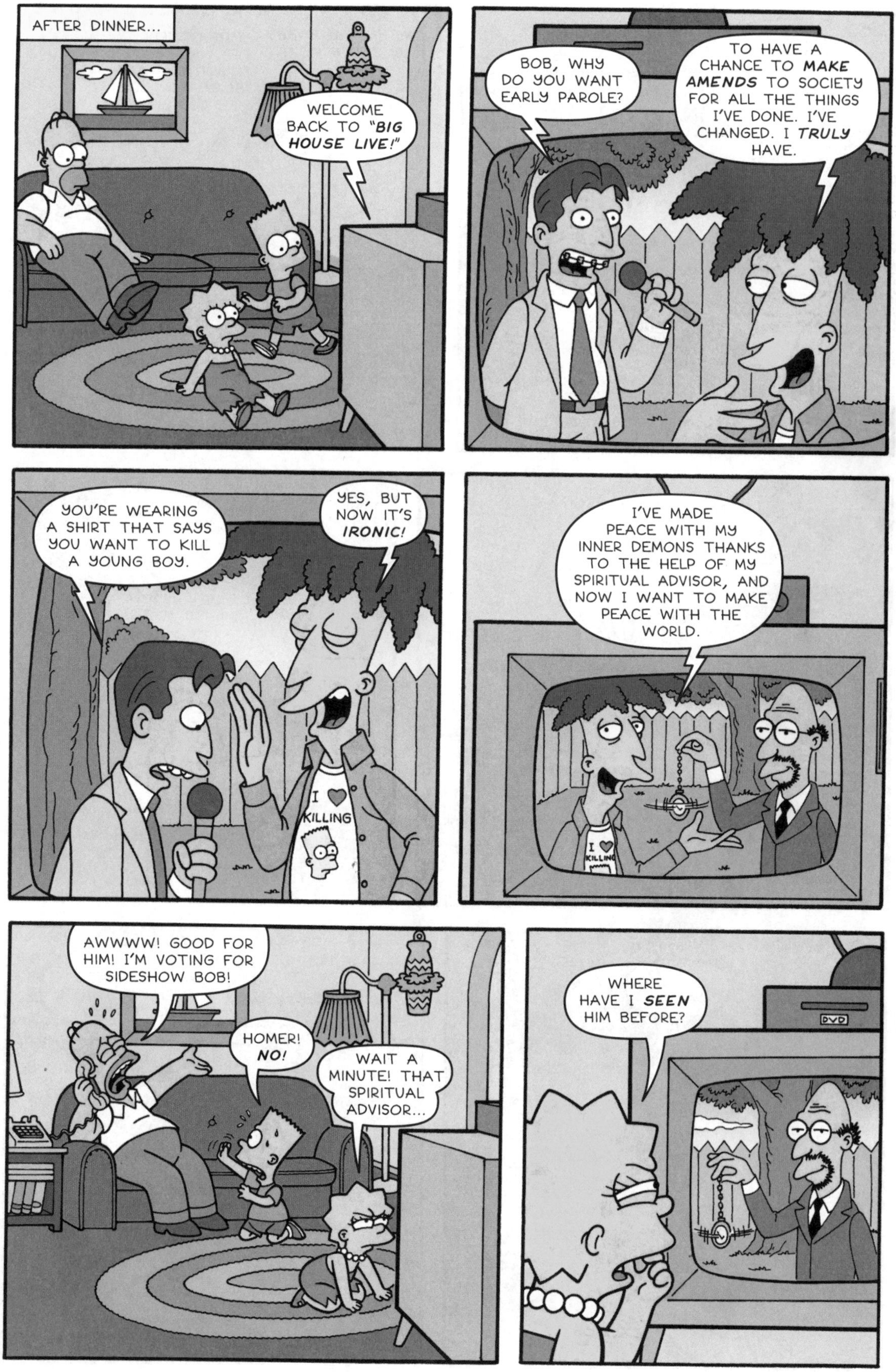
AFTER DINNER...
WELCOME BACK TO "BIG HOUSE LIVE!"
BOB, WHY DO YOU WANT EARLY PAROLE?
TO HAVE A CHANCE TO MAKE AMENDS TO SOCIETY FOR ALL THE THINGS I'VE DONE. I'VE CHANGED. I TRULY HAVE.
YOU'RE WEARING A SHIRT THAT SAYS YOU WANT TO KILL A YOUNG BOY.
YES, BUT NOW IT'S IRONIC!
I ♥ KILLING
I'VE MADE PEACE WITH MY INNER DEMONS THANKS TO THE HELP OF MY SPIRITUAL ADVISOR, AND NOW I WANT TO MAKE PEACE WITH THE WORLD.
AWWWW! GOOD FOR HIM! I'M VOTING FOR SIDESHOW BOB!
HOMER! NO!
WAIT A MINUTE! THAT SPIRITUAL ADVISOR...
WHERE HAVE I SEEN HIM BEFORE?
DVD

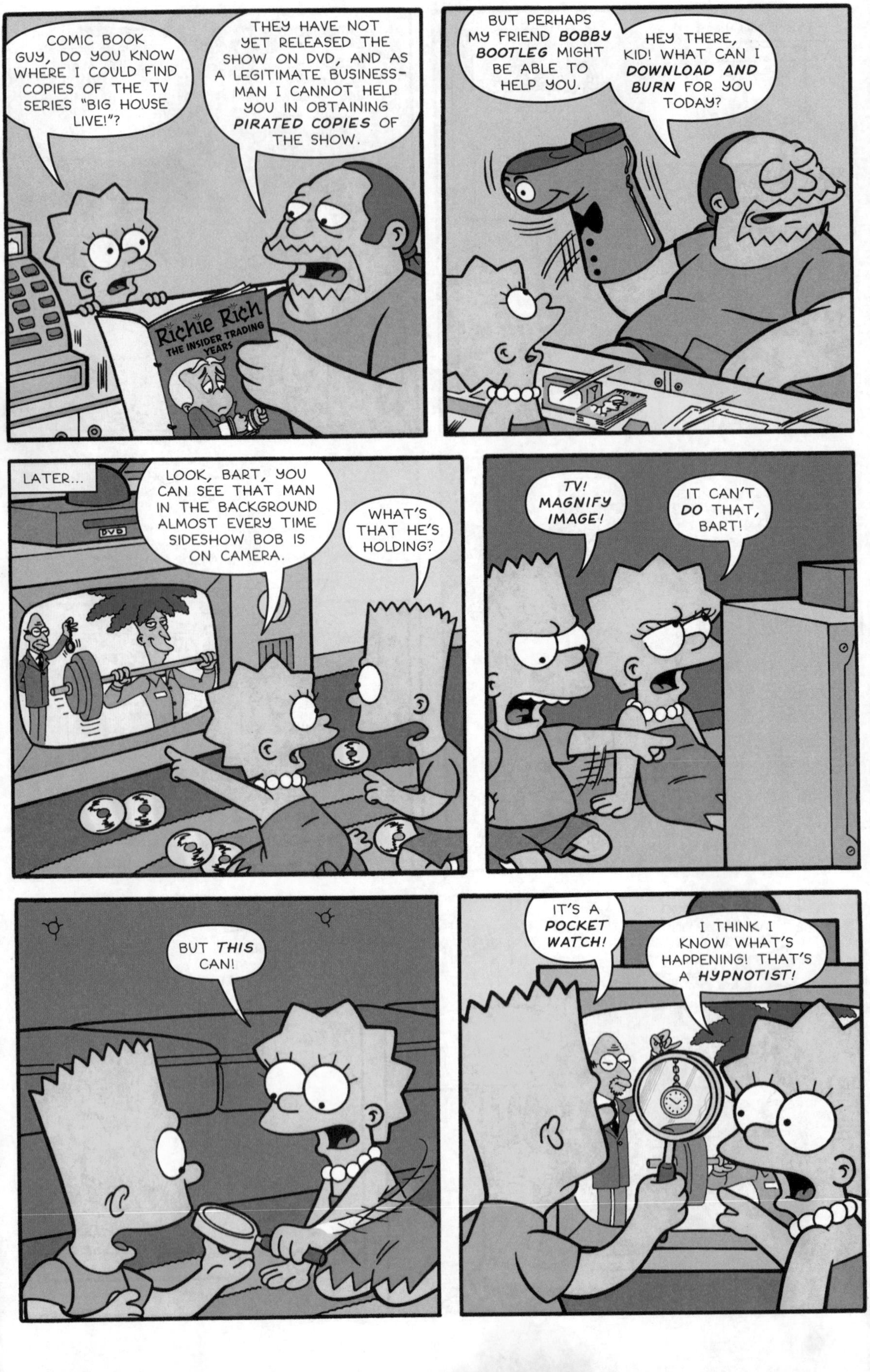
COMIC BOOK GUY, DO YOU KNOW WHERE I COULD FIND COPIES OF THE TV SERIES "BIG HOUSE LIVE!"?
THEY HAVE NOT YET RELEASED THE SHOW ON DVD, AND AS A LEGITIMATE BUSINESS-MAN I CANNOT HELP YOU IN OBTAINING **PIRATED COPIES** OF THE SHOW.
Richie Rich
THE INSIDER TRADING YEARS
BUT PERHAPS MY FRIEND **BOBBY BOOTLEG** MIGHT BE ABLE TO HELP YOU.
HEY THERE, KID! WHAT CAN I **DOWNLOAD AND BURN** FOR YOU TODAY?
LATER...
LOOK, BART, YOU CAN SEE THAT MAN IN THE BACKGROUND ALMOST EVERY TIME SIDESHOW BOB IS ON CAMERA.
WHAT'S THAT HE'S HOLDING?
DVD
TV! MAGNIFY IMAGE!
IT CAN'T ***DO*** THAT, BART!
BUT ***THIS*** CAN!
IT'S A ***POCKET WATCH!***
I THINK I KNOW WHAT'S HAPPENING! THAT'S A ***HYPNOTIST!***

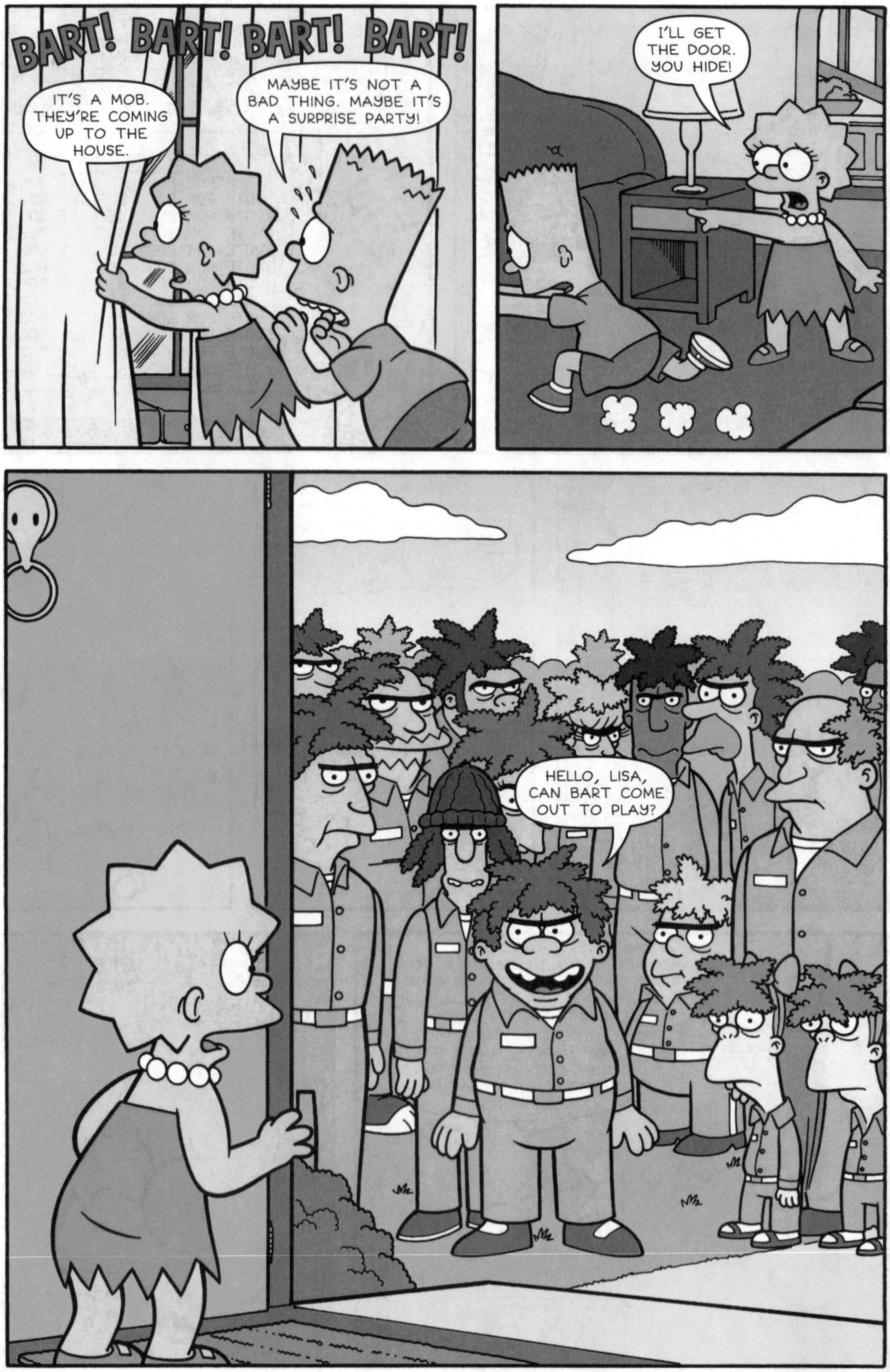
BART! BART! BART! BART!
IT'S A MOB. THEY'RE COMING UP TO THE HOUSE.
MAYBE IT'S NOT A BAD THING. MAYBE IT'S A SURPRISE PARTY!
I'LL GET THE DOOR. YOU HIDE!
HELLO, LISA, CAN BART COME OUT TO PLAY?

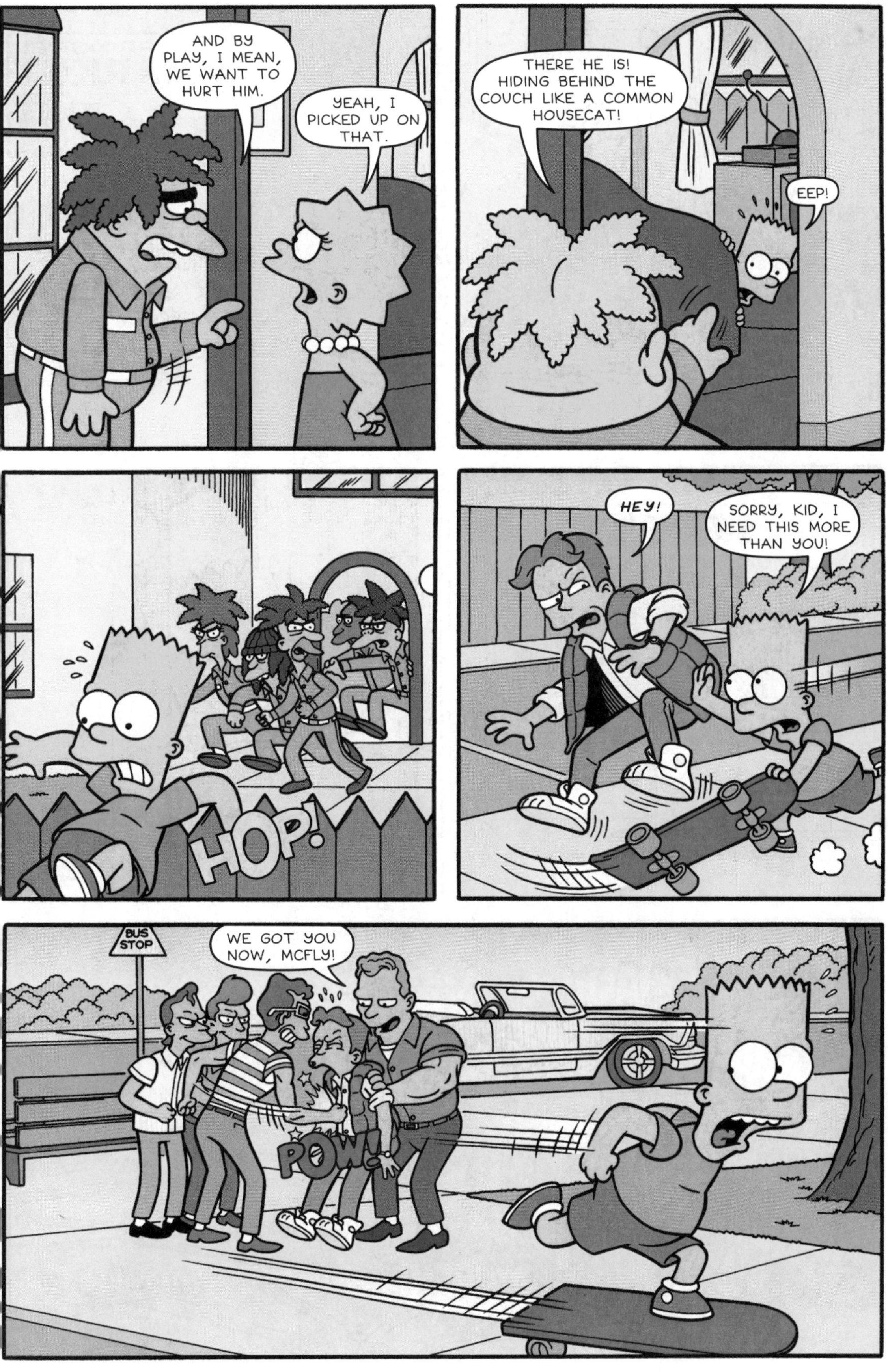
AND BY PLAY, I MEAN, WE WANT TO HURT HIM.
YEAH, I PICKED UP ON THAT.
THERE HE IS! HIDING BEHIND THE COUCH LIKE A COMMON HOUSECAT!
EEP!
HOP!
HEY!
SORRY, KID, I NEED THIS MORE THAN YOU!
BUS STOP
WE GOT YOU NOW, MCFLY!
POW!

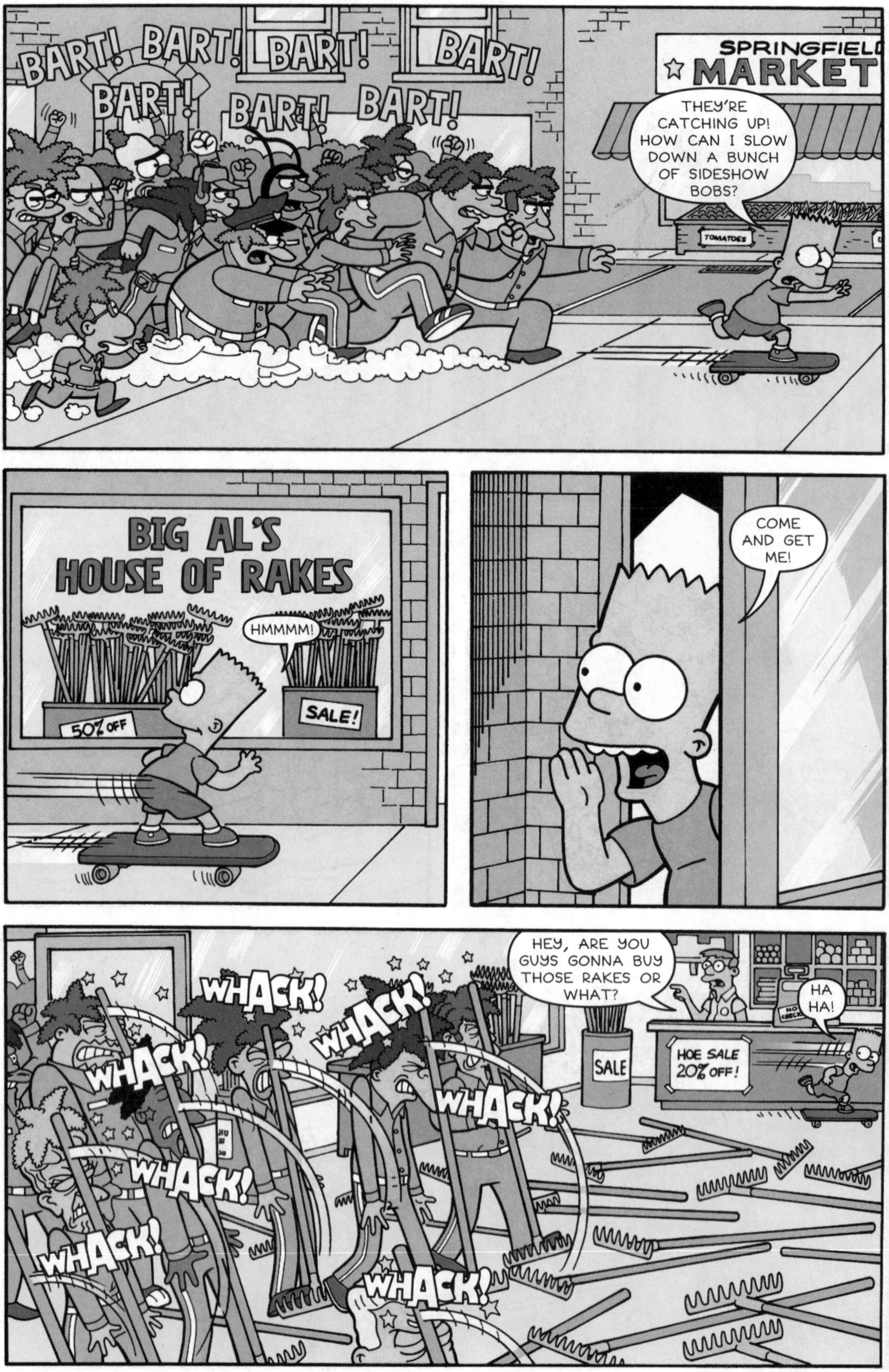
BART! BART! BART! BART!
BART! BART! BART!
SPRINGFIELD MARKET
THEY'RE CATCHING UP! HOW CAN I SLOW DOWN A BUNCH OF SIDESHOW BOBS?
TOMATOES
BIG AL'S HOUSE OF RAKES
HMMMM!
50% OFF
SALE!
COME AND GET ME!
HEY, ARE YOU GUYS GONNA BUY THOSE RAKES OR WHAT?
HA HA!
SALE
HOE SALE 20% OFF!
WHACK!
WHACK!
WHACK!
WHACK!
WHACK!
WHACK!
WHACK!

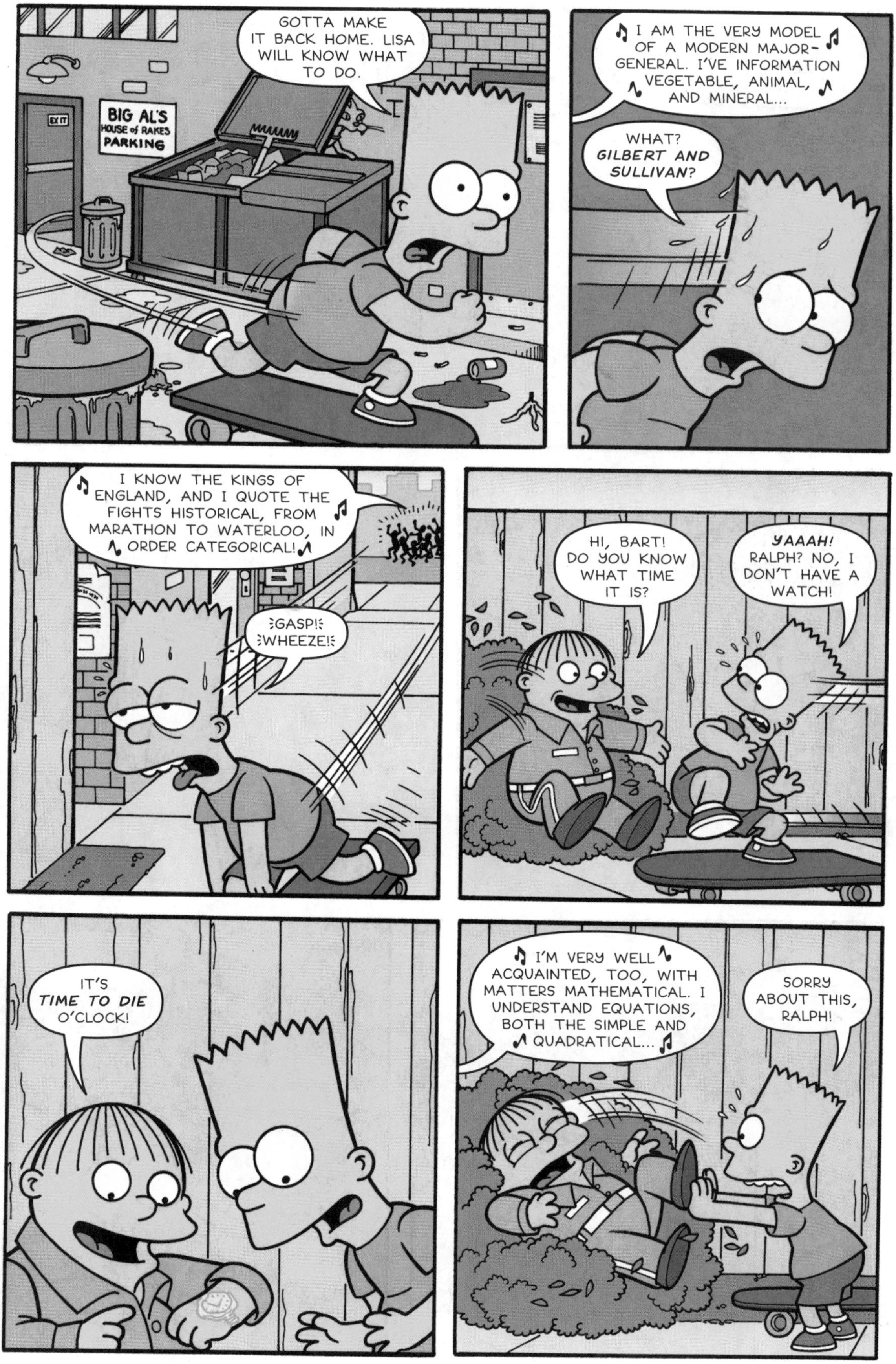
GOTTA MAKE IT BACK HOME. LISA WILL KNOW WHAT TO DO.
BIG AL'S HOUSE of RAKES PARKING
EXIT
I AM THE VERY MODEL OF A MODERN MAJOR-GENERAL. I'VE INFORMATION VEGETABLE, ANIMAL, AND MINERAL...
WHAT? *GILBERT AND SULLIVAN?*
I KNOW THE KINGS OF ENGLAND, AND I QUOTE THE FIGHTS HISTORICAL, FROM MARATHON TO WATERLOO, IN ORDER CATEGORICAL!
GASP! WHEEZE!
HI, BART! DO YOU KNOW WHAT TIME IT IS?
YAAAH! RALPH? NO, I DON'T HAVE A WATCH!
IT'S *TIME TO DIE* O'CLOCK!
I'M VERY WELL ACQUAINTED, TOO, WITH MATTERS MATHEMATICAL. I UNDERSTAND EQUATIONS, BOTH THE SIMPLE AND QUADRATICAL...
SORRY ABOUT THIS, RALPH!

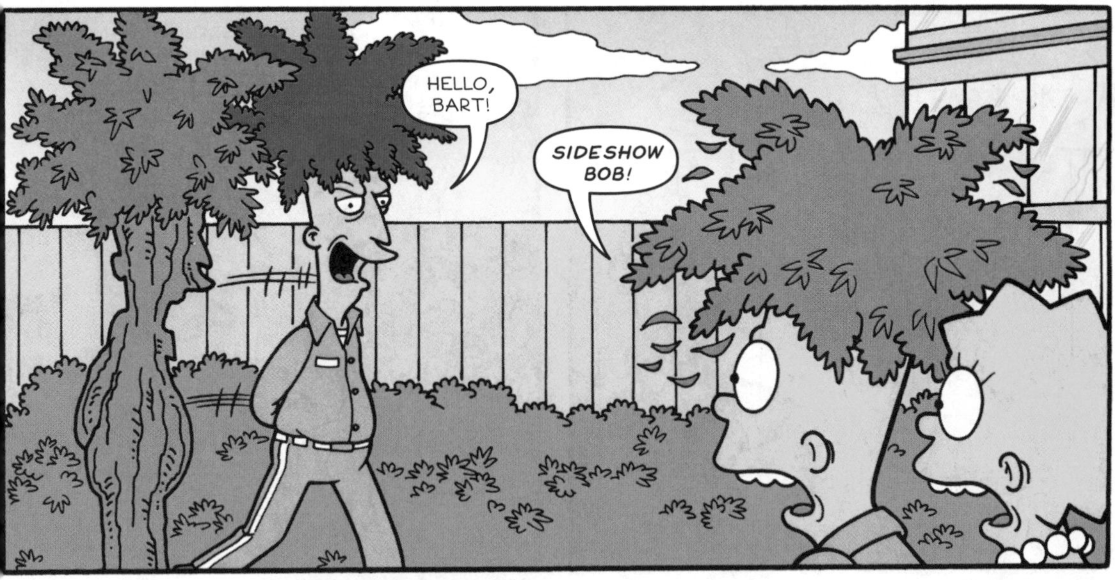
HELLO, BART!
SIDESHOW BOB!

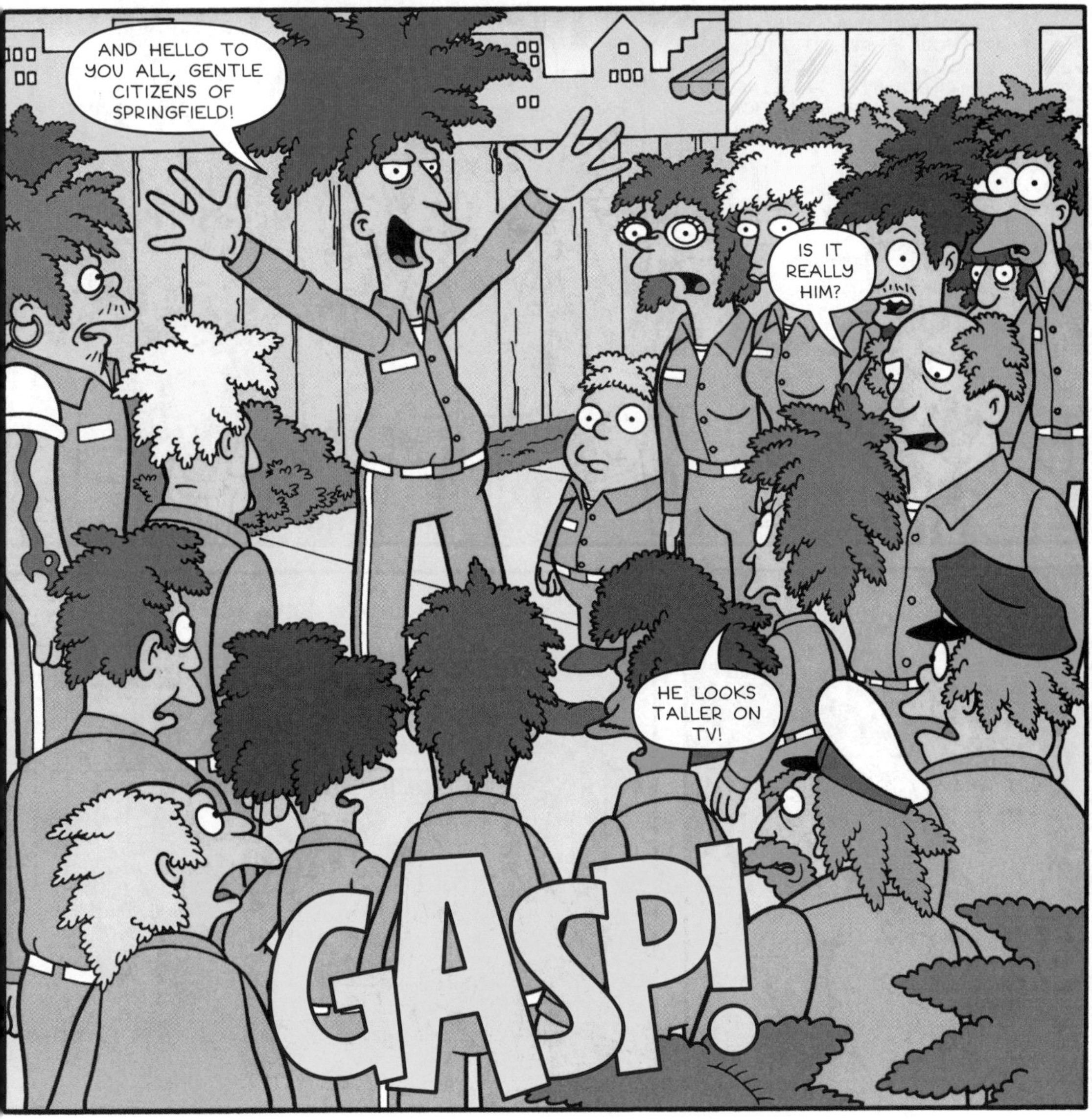
AND HELLO TO YOU ALL, GENTLE CITIZENS OF SPRINGFIELD!
IS IT REALLY HIM?
HE LOOKS TALLER ON TV!
GASP!

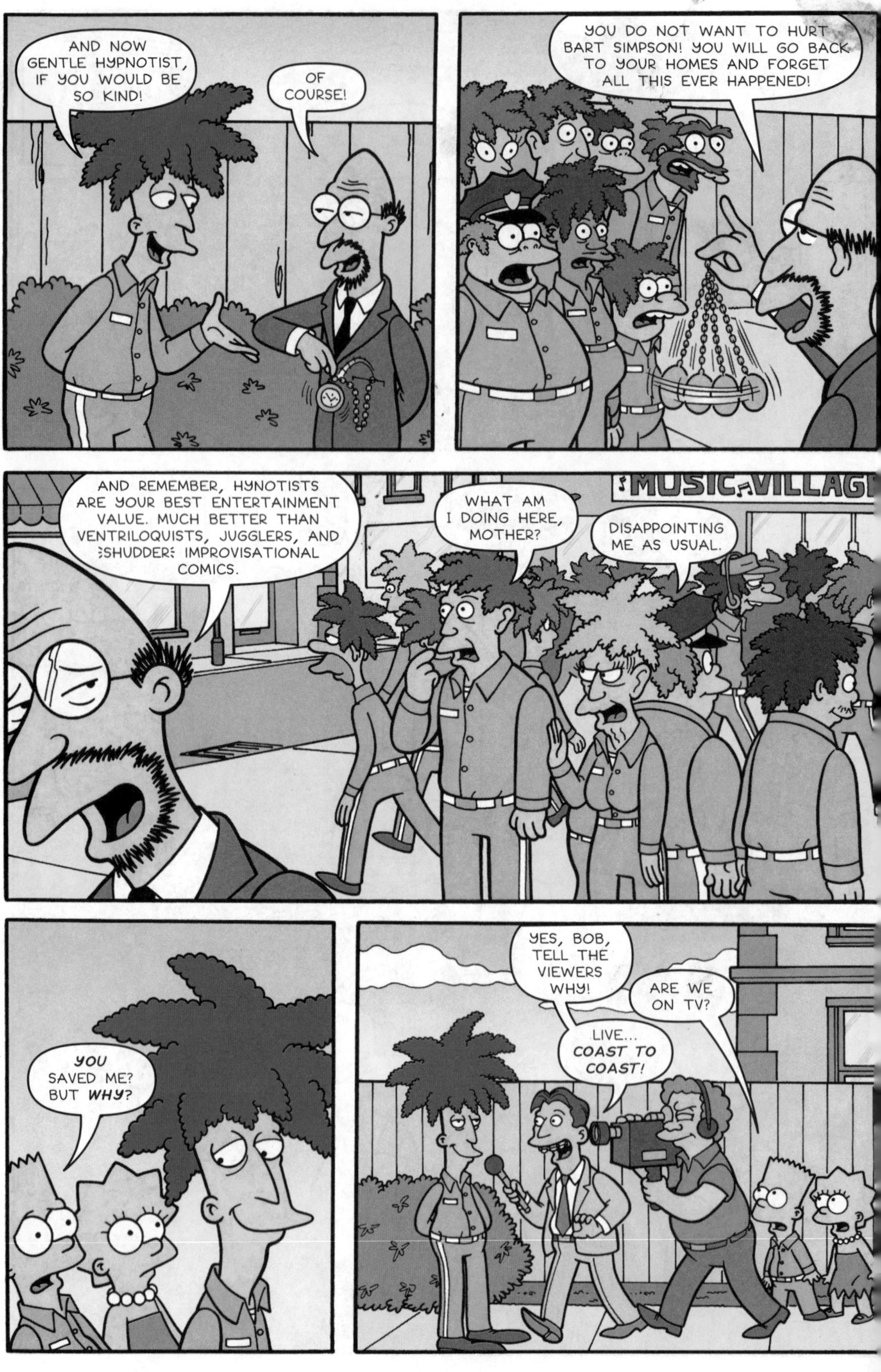
AND NOW GENTLE HYPNOTIST, IF YOU WOULD BE SO KIND!
OF COURSE!
YOU DO NOT WANT TO HURT BART SIMPSON! YOU WILL GO BACK TO YOUR HOMES AND FORGET ALL THIS EVER HAPPENED!
AND REMEMBER, HYNOTISTS ARE YOUR BEST ENTERTAINMENT VALUE. MUCH BETTER THAN VENTRILOQUISTS, JUGGLERS, AND ⁝SHUDDER⁝ IMPROVISATIONAL COMICS.
MUSIC VILLAGE
WHAT AM I DOING HERE, MOTHER?
DISAPPOINTING ME AS USUAL.
YOU SAVED ME? BUT WHY?
YES, BOB, TELL THE VIEWERS WHY!
ARE WE ON TV?
LIVE... COAST TO COAST!

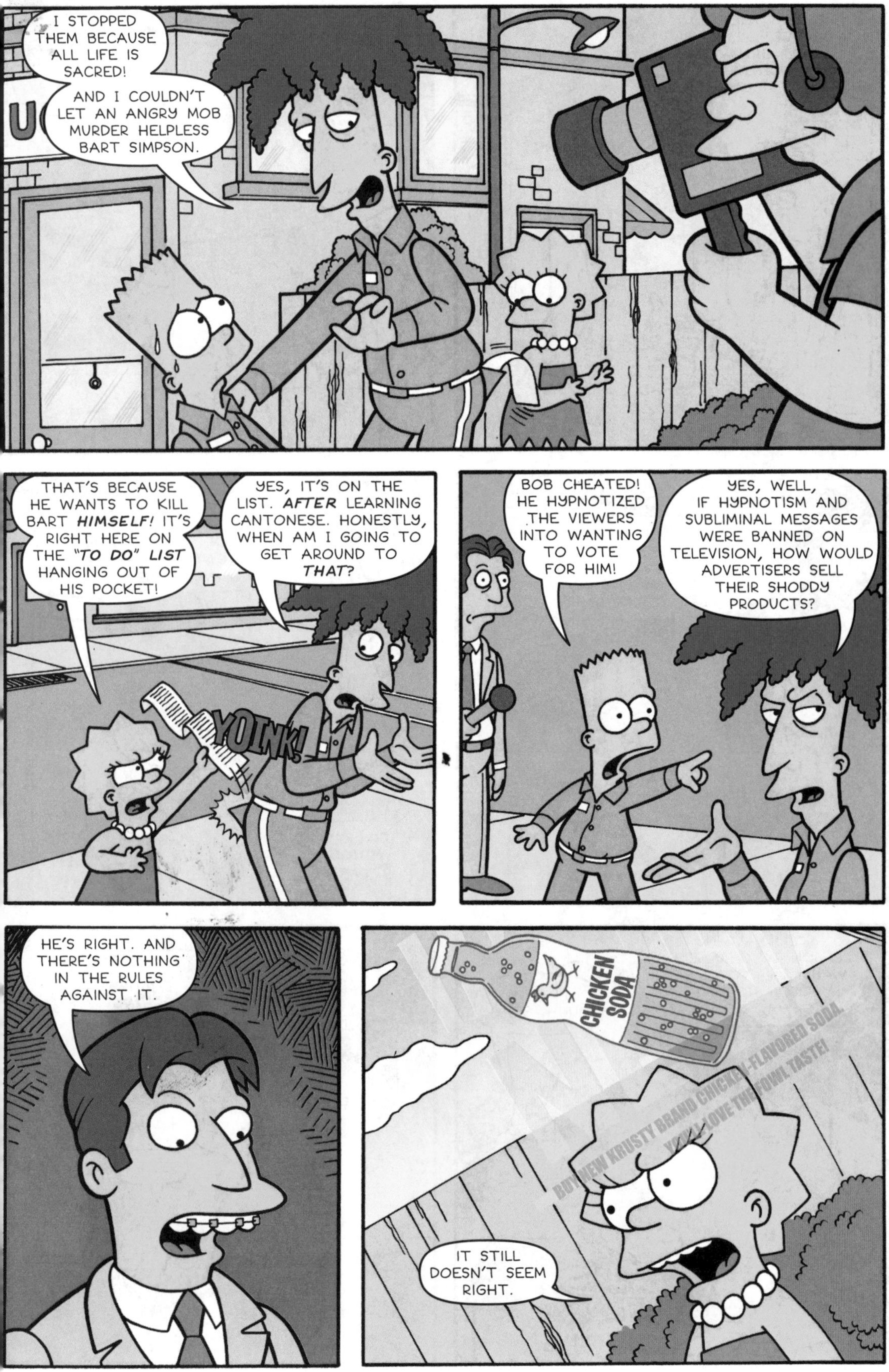

I STOPPED THEM BECAUSE ALL LIFE IS SACRED!
AND I COULDN'T LET AN ANGRY MOB MURDER HELPLESS BART SIMPSON.
THAT'S BECAUSE HE WANTS TO KILL BART *HIMSELF!* IT'S RIGHT HERE ON THE *"TO DO" LIST* HANGING OUT OF HIS POCKET!
YES, IT'S ON THE LIST. *AFTER* LEARNING CANTONESE. HONESTLY, WHEN AM I GOING TO GET AROUND TO *THAT*?
YOINK!
BOB CHEATED! HE HYPNOTIZED THE VIEWERS INTO WANTING TO VOTE FOR HIM!
YES, WELL, IF HYPNOTISM AND SUBLIMINAL MESSAGES WERE BANNED ON TELEVISION, HOW WOULD ADVERTISERS SELL THEIR SHODDY PRODUCTS?
HE'S RIGHT. AND THERE'S NOTHING IN THE RULES AGAINST IT.
CHICKEN SODA
BUY NEW KRUSTY BRAND CHICKEN-FLAVORED SODA.
YOU'LL LOVE THE FOWL TASTE!
IT STILL DOESN'T SEEM RIGHT.

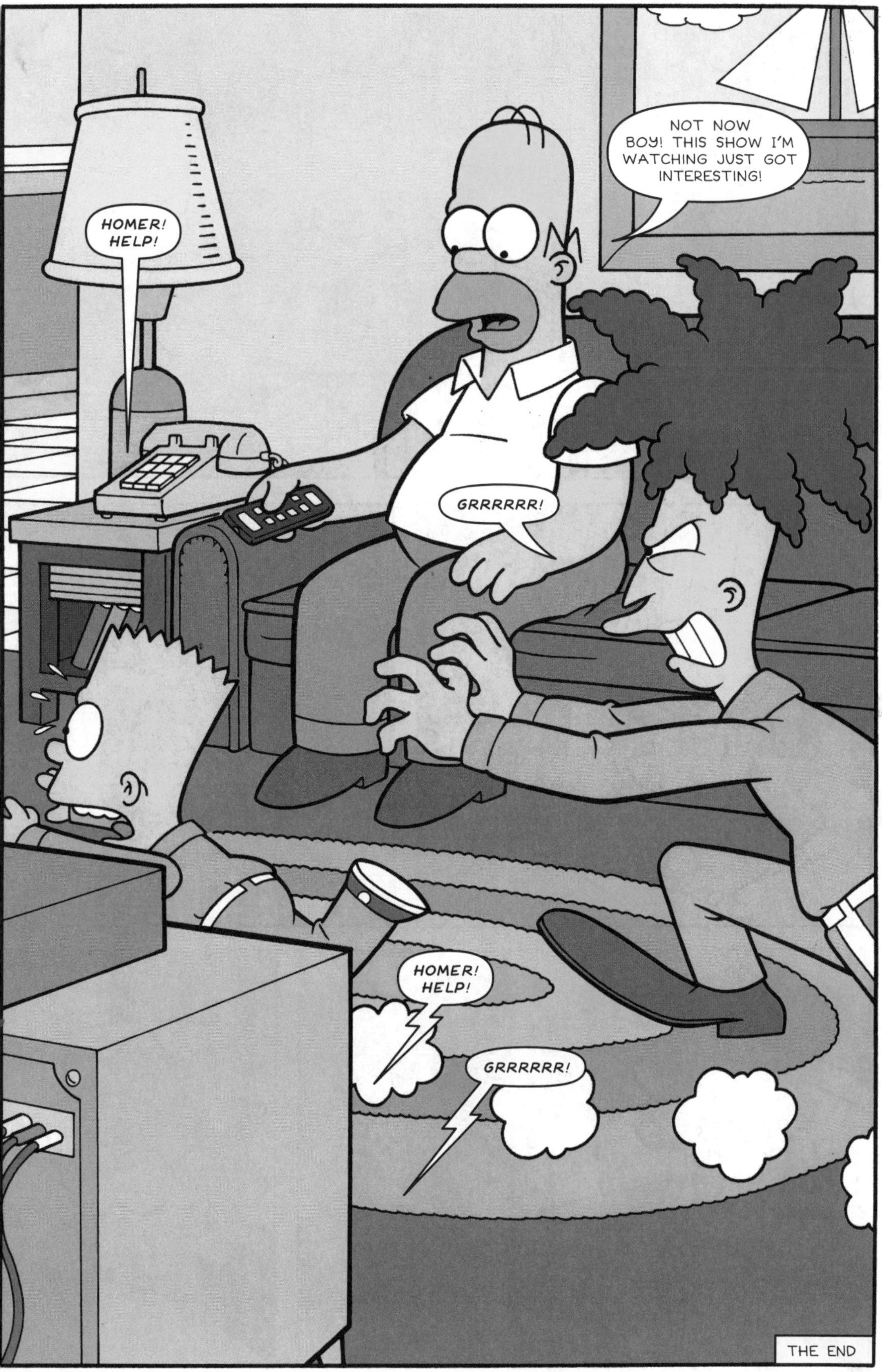
HOMER! HELP!
NOT NOW BOY! THIS SHOW I'M WATCHING JUST GOT INTERESTING!
GRRRRRR!
HOMER! HELP!
GRRRRRR!
THE END

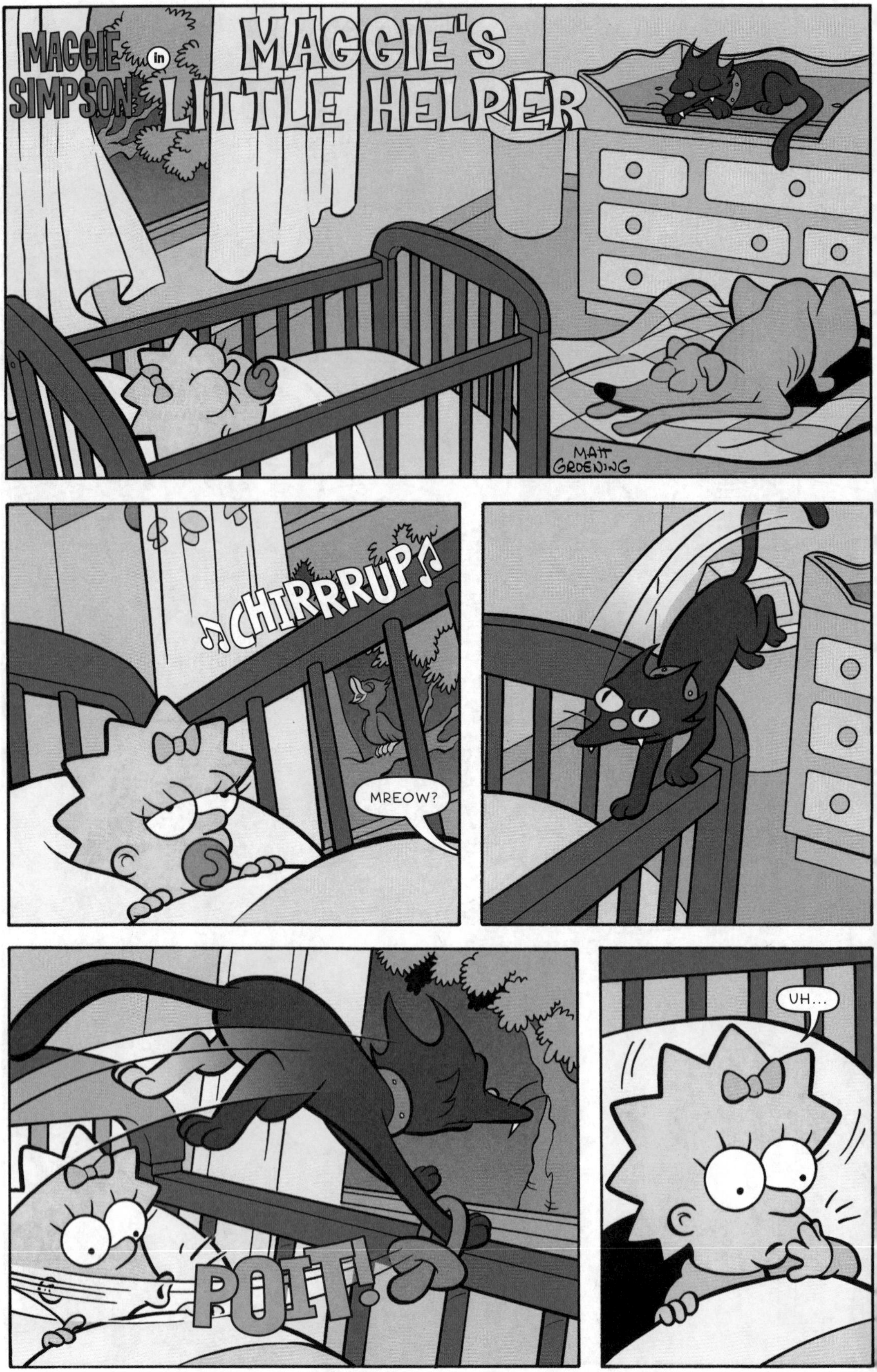
MAGGIE SIMPSON in
MAGGIE'S LITTLE HELPER
MATT GROENING
CHIRRRUP
MREOW?
POIT!
UH...

TOM PEYER SCRIPT | *CARLOS VALENTI* PENCILS | *ANDREW PEPOY* INKS | *ART VILLANUEVA* COLORS | *KAREN BATES* LETTERS | *BILL MORRISON* EDITOR

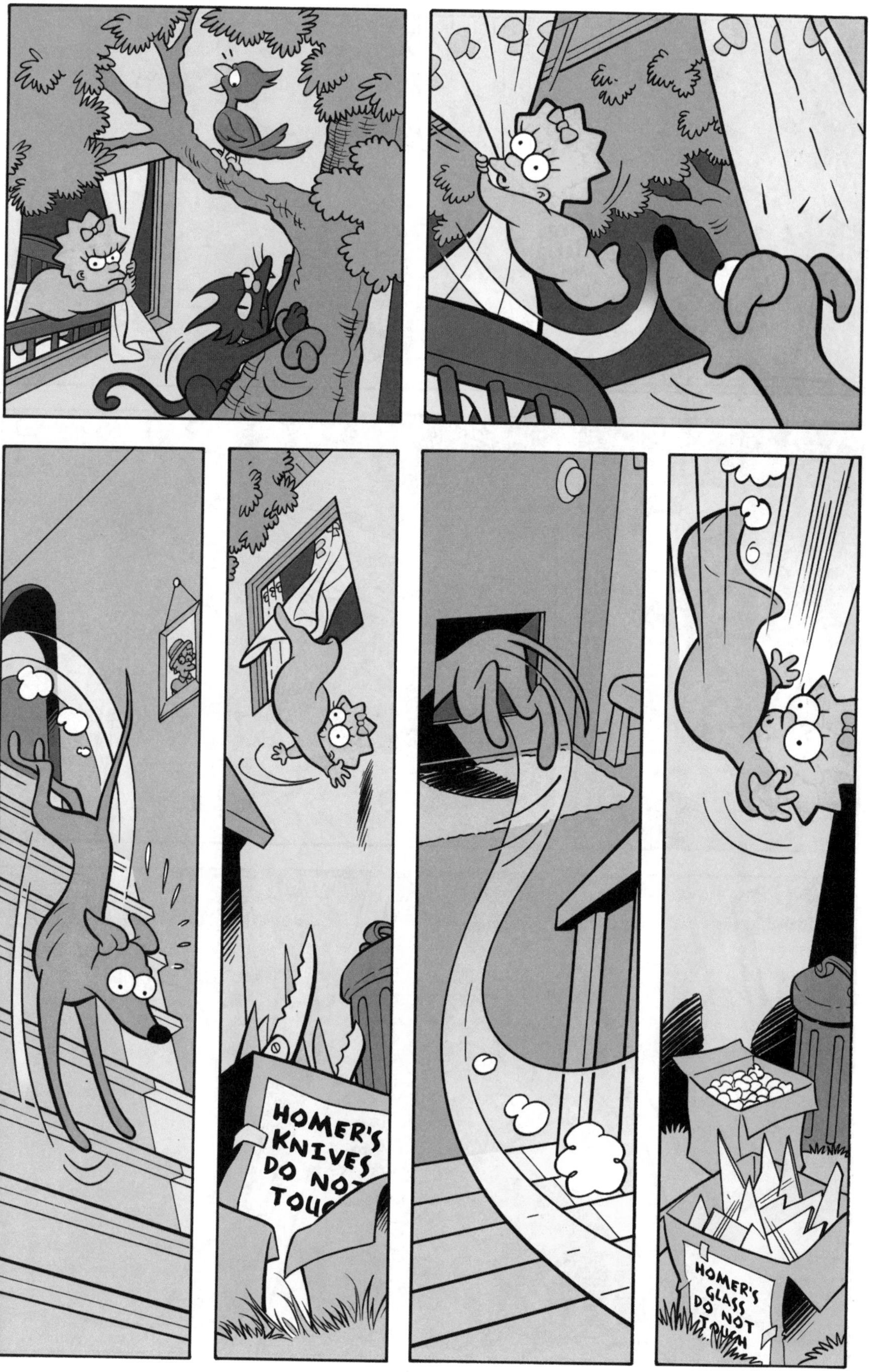
HOMER'S KNIVES DO NOT TOUC
HOMER'S GLASS DO NOT TOUCH

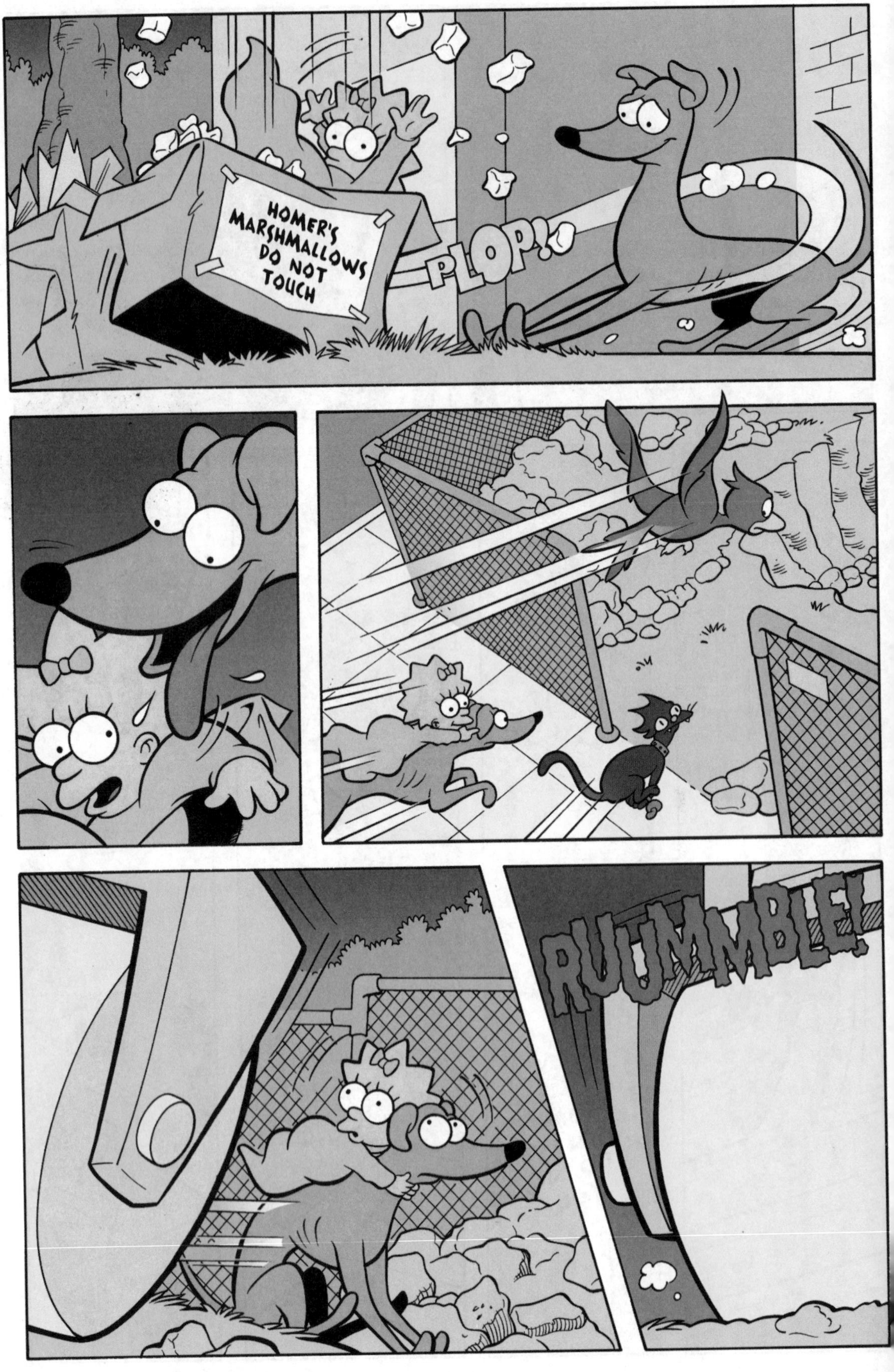
HOMER'S MARSHMALLOWS DO NOT TOUCH
PLOP!
RUUMMBLE!

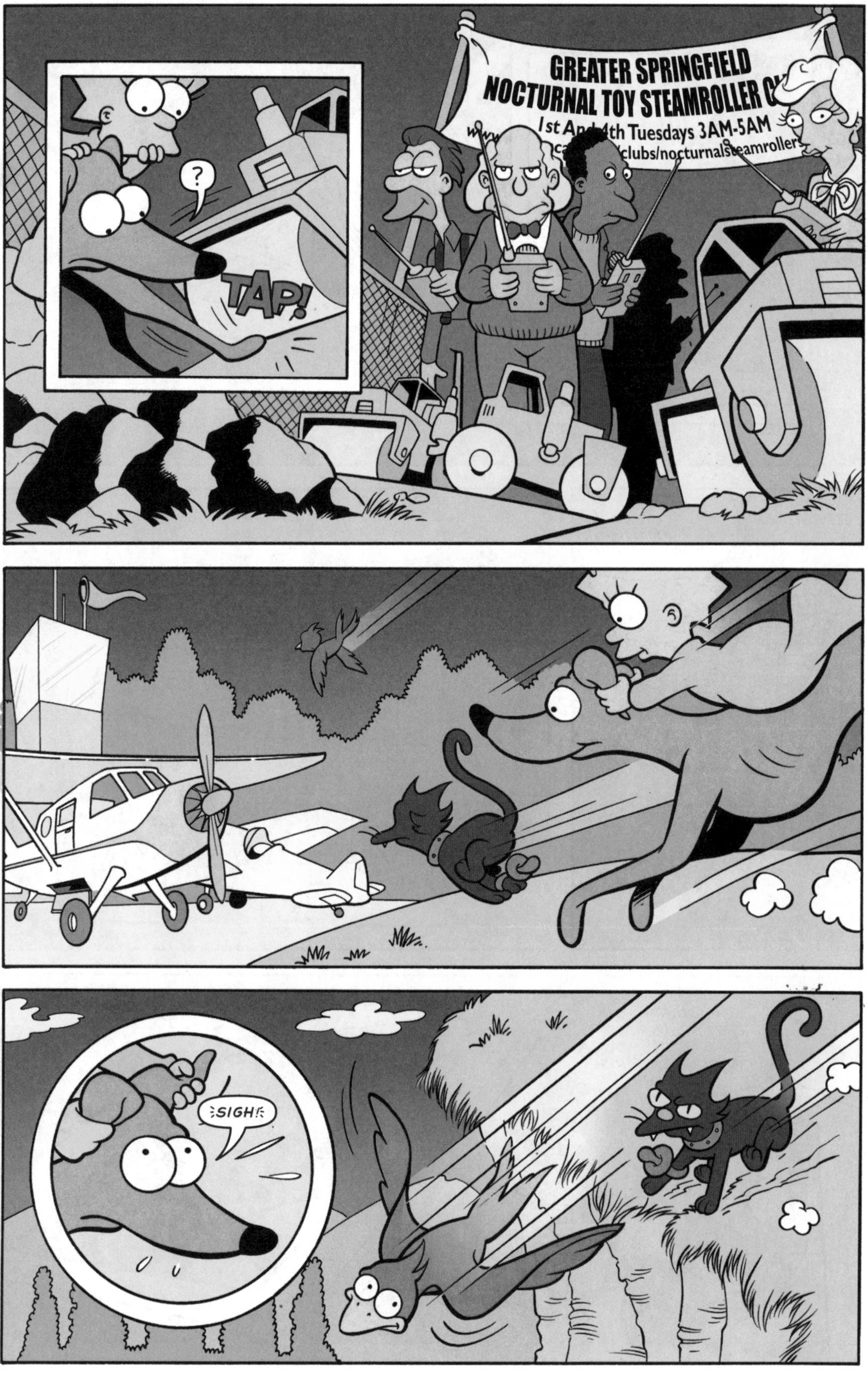
?
TAP!
GREATER SPRINGFIELD
NOCTURNAL TOY STEAMROLLER C
1st A 4th Tuesdays 3AM-5AM
/clubs/nocturnalsteamrollers
SIGH!

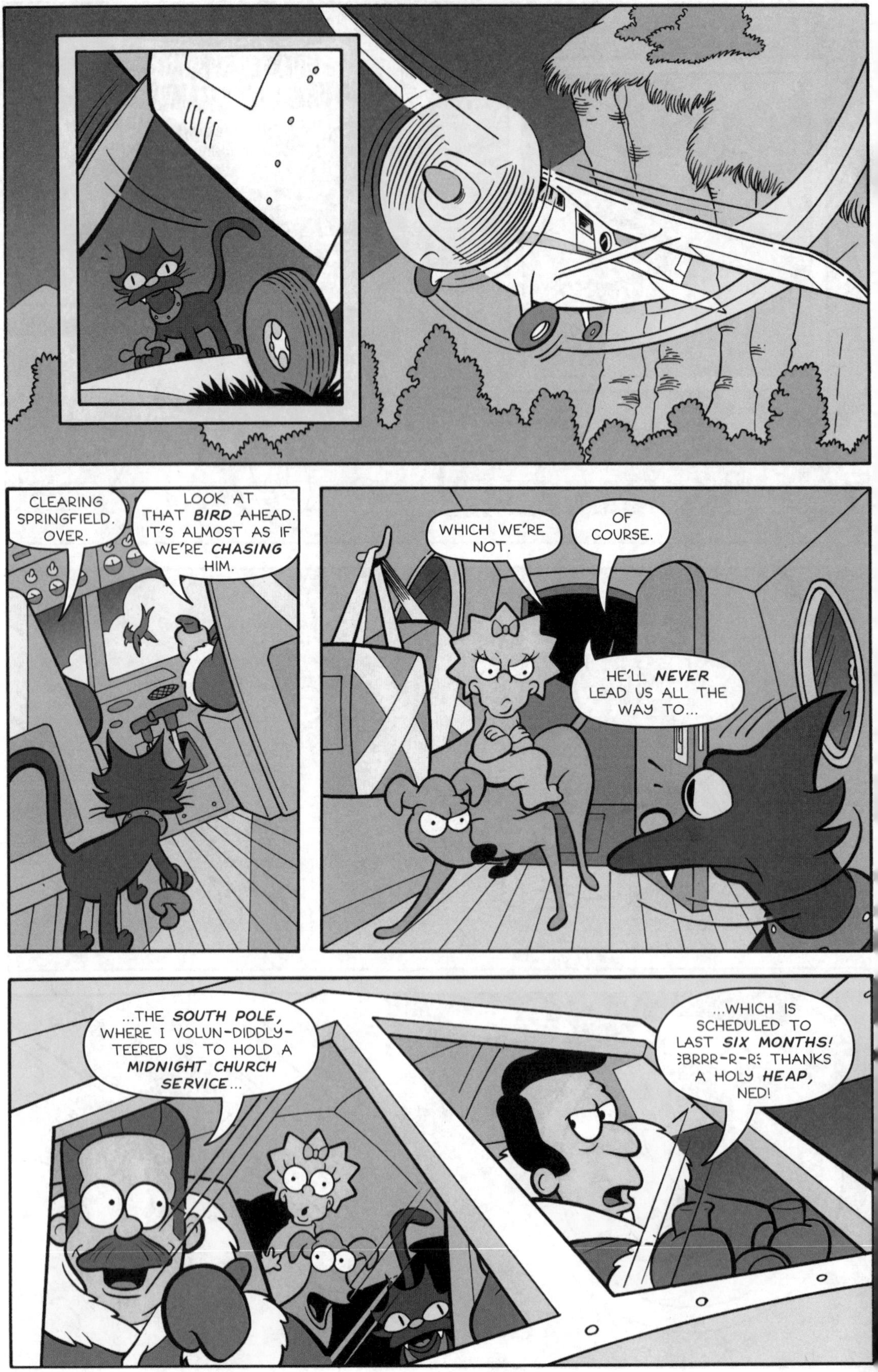

CLEARING SPRINGFIELD. OVER.
LOOK AT THAT BIRD AHEAD. IT'S ALMOST AS IF WE'RE CHASING HIM.
WHICH WE'RE NOT.
OF COURSE.
HE'LL NEVER LEAD US ALL THE WAY TO...
...THE SOUTH POLE, WHERE I VOLUN-DIDDLY-TEERED US TO HOLD A MIDNIGHT CHURCH SERVICE...
...WHICH IS SCHEDULED TO LAST SIX MONTHS! BRRR-R-R THANKS A HOLY HEAP, NED!

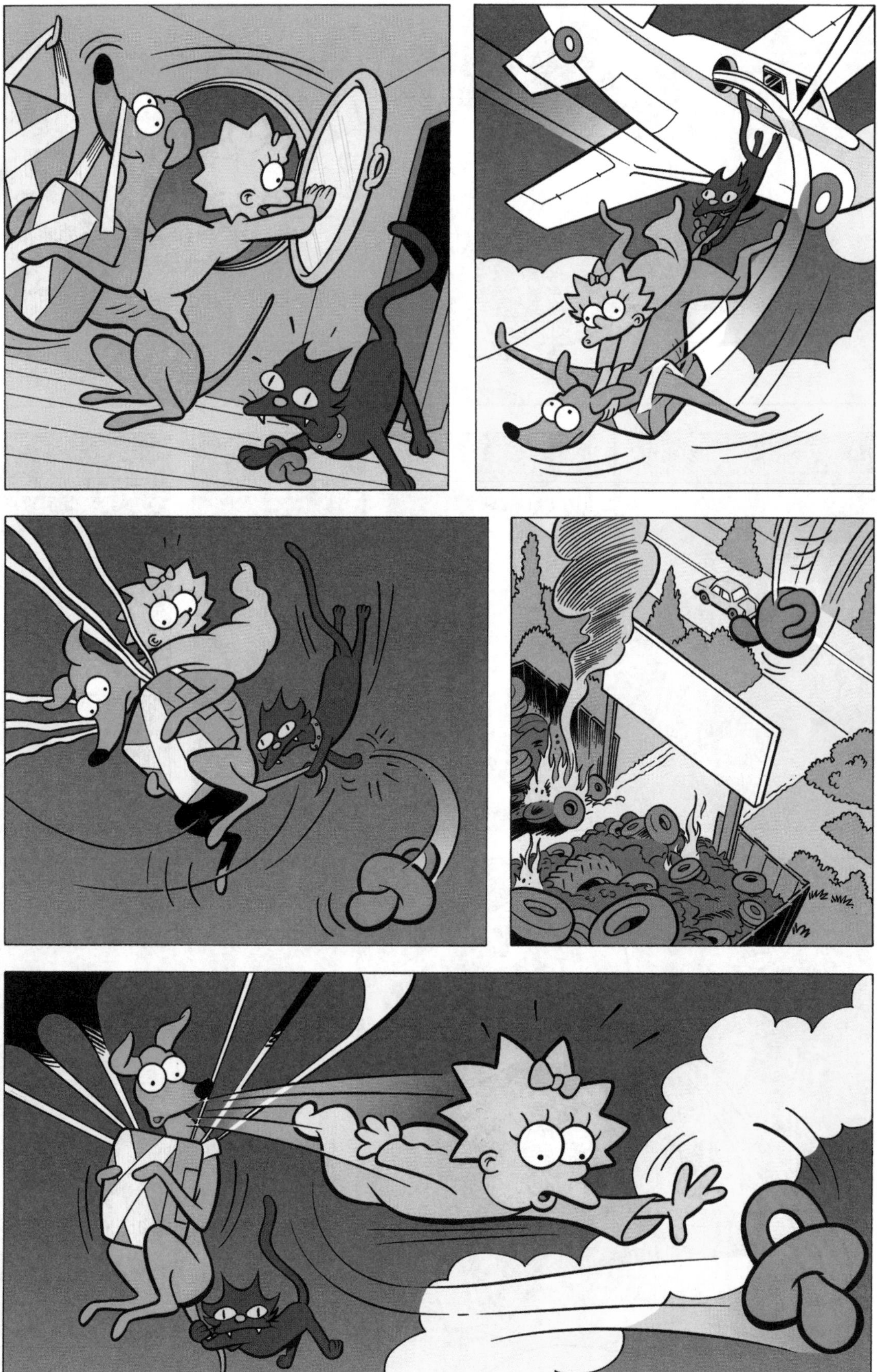

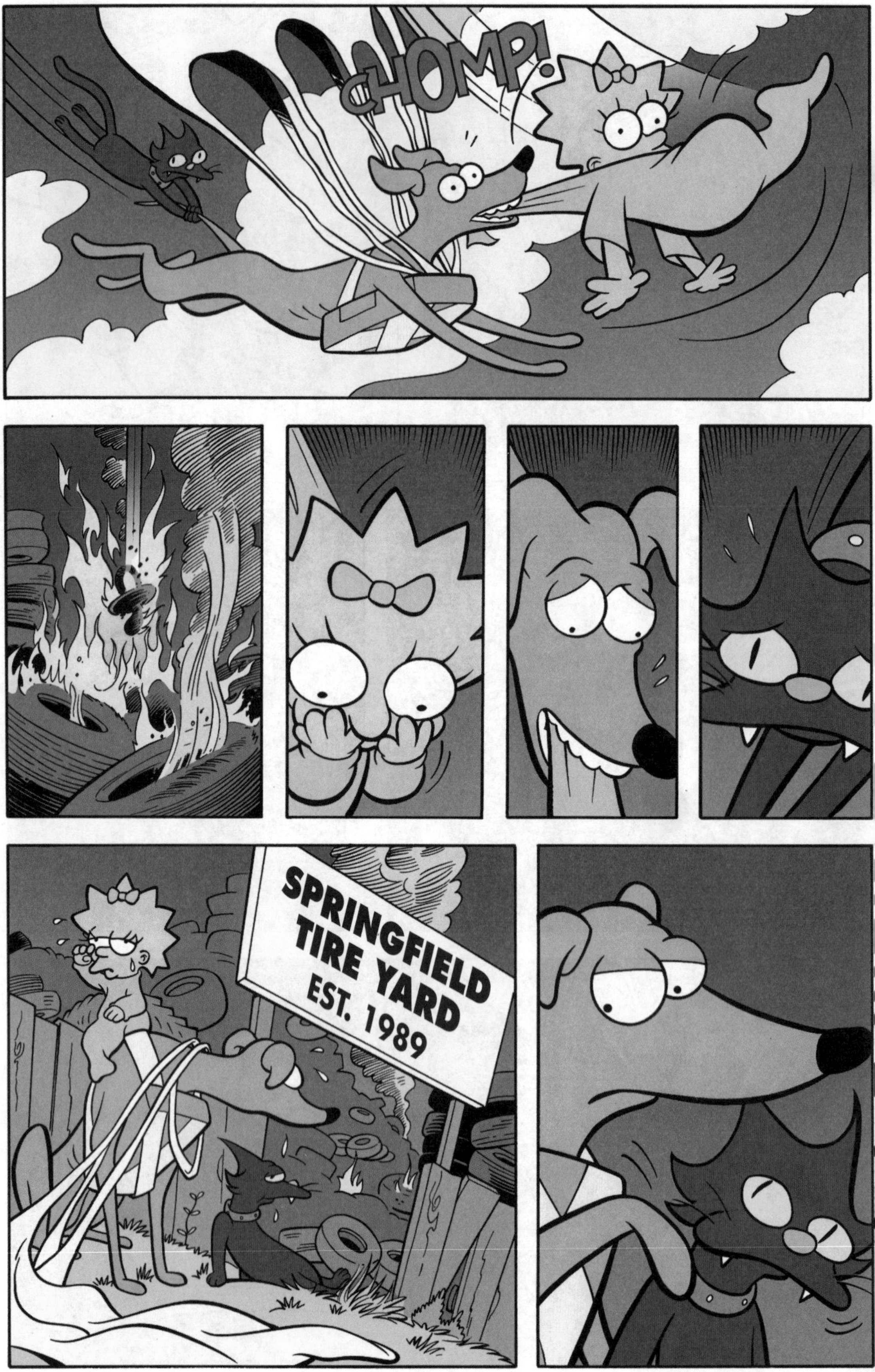
CHOMP!
SPRINGFIELD
TIRE YARD
EST. 1989

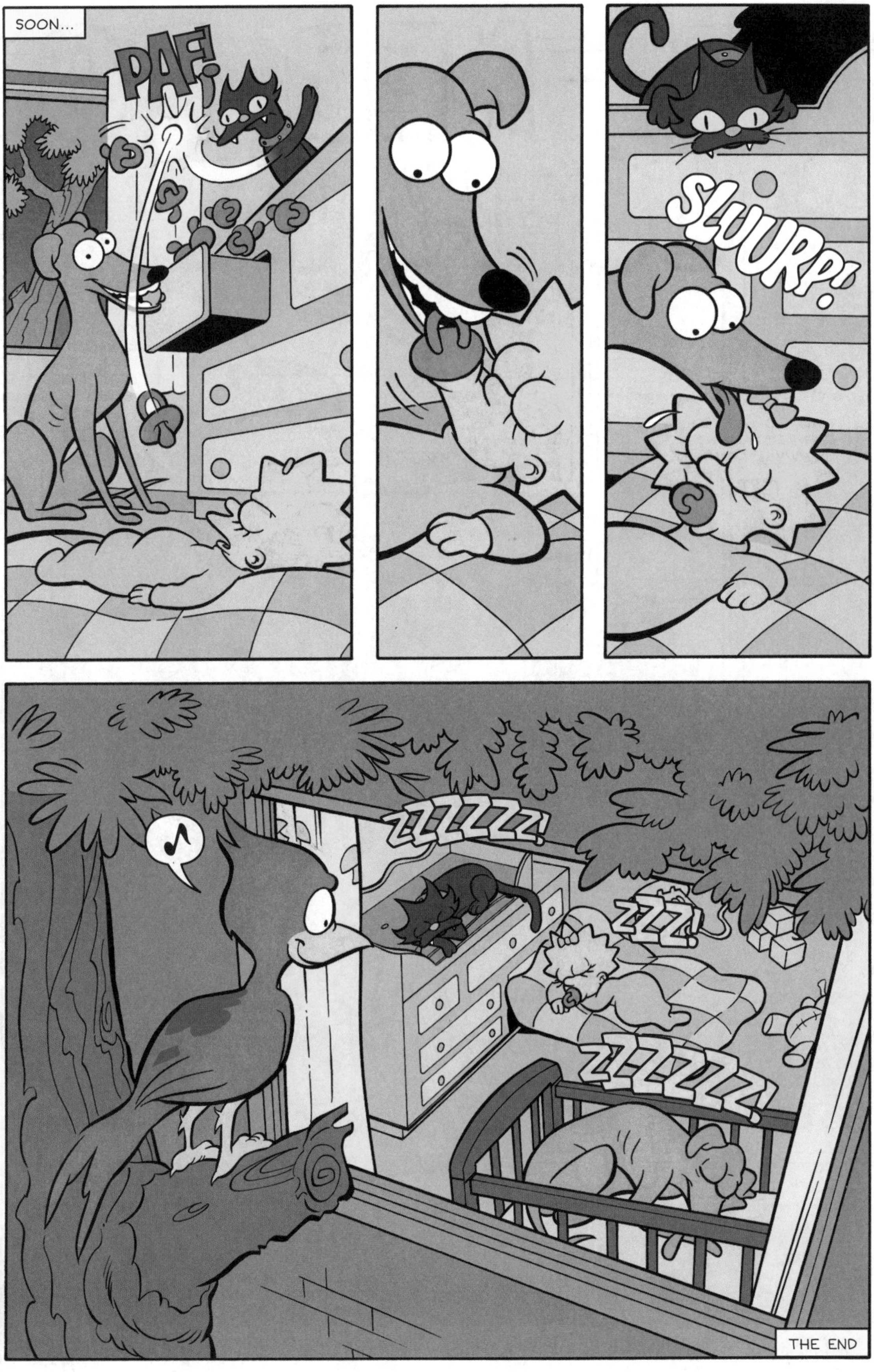
SOON...
PAF!
SLUURP!
♪
ZZZZZZ!
ZZZ!
ZZZZZZ!
THE END

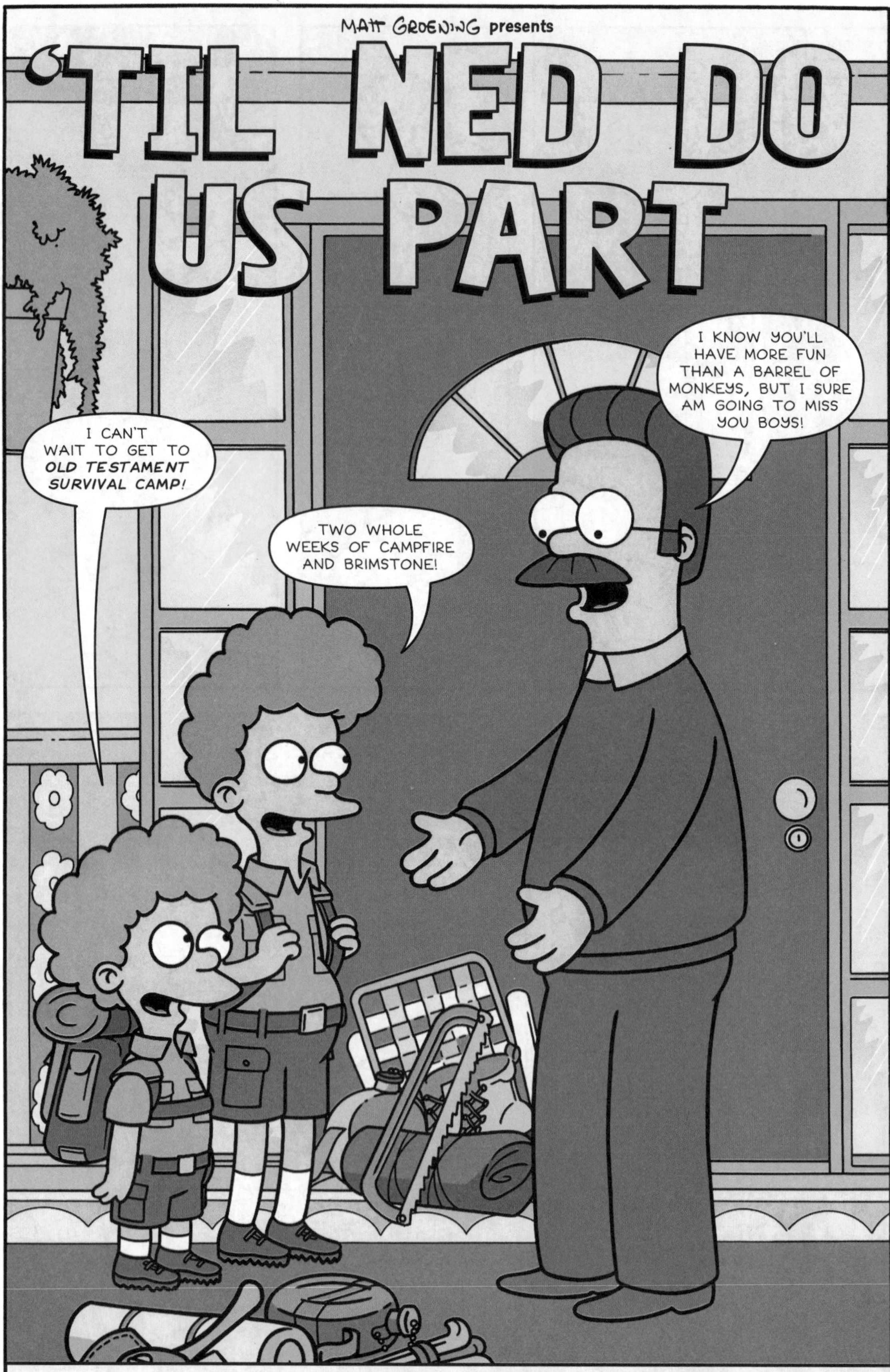
MATT GROENING presents
'TIL NED DO US PART
I CAN'T WAIT TO GET TO OLD TESTAMENT SURVIVAL CAMP!
TWO WHOLE WEEKS OF CAMPFIRE AND BRIMSTONE!
I KNOW YOU'LL HAVE MORE FUN THAN A BARREL OF MONKEYS, BUT I SURE AM GOING TO MISS YOU BOYS!

MARY TRAINOR SCRIPT · JOHN COSTANZA PENCILS · PHYLLIS NOVIN INKS · ART VILLANUEVA COLORS · KAREN BATES LETTERS · BILL MORRISON EDITOR

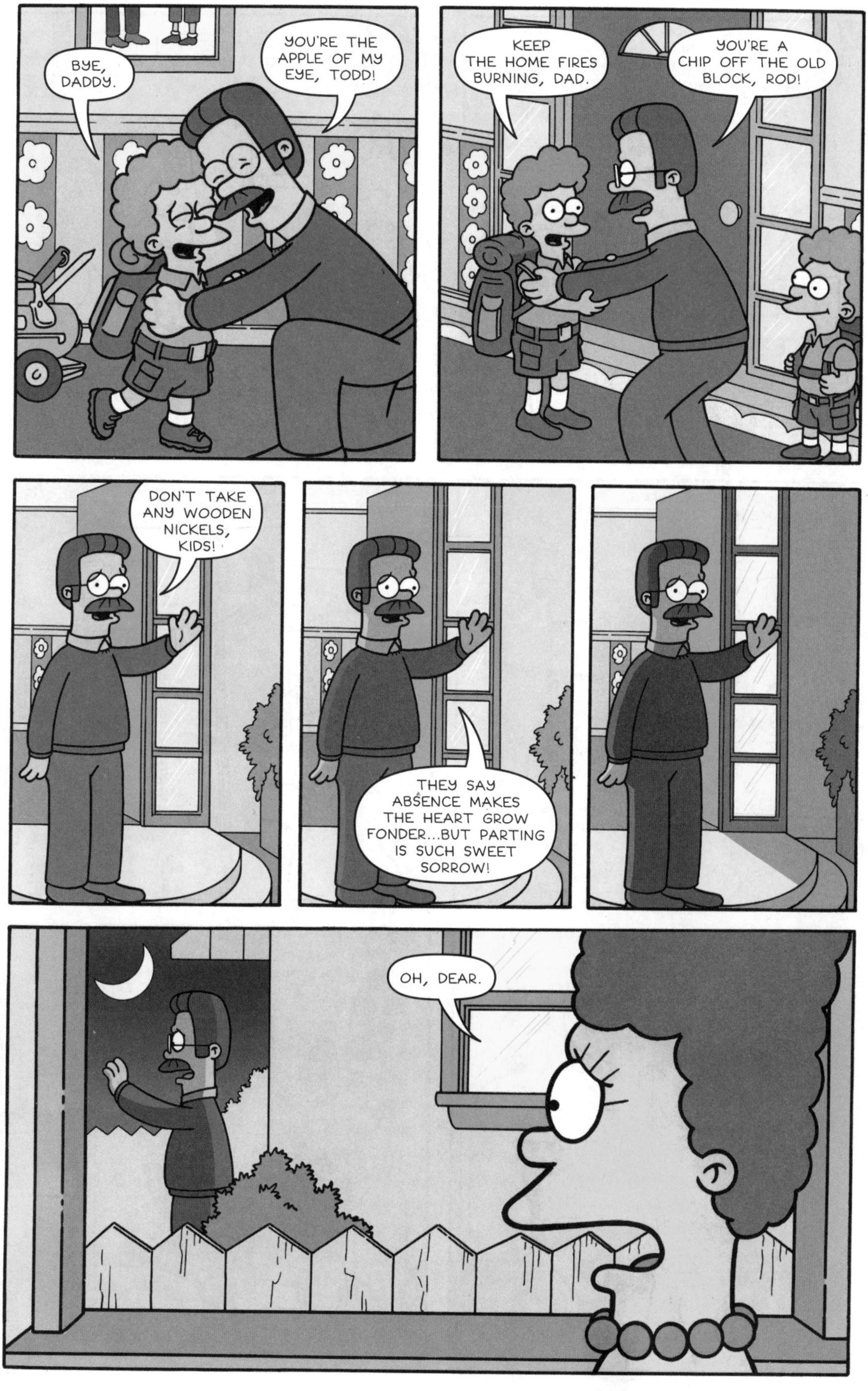

BYE, DADDY.
YOU'RE THE APPLE OF MY EYE, TODD!
KEEP THE HOME FIRES BURNING, DAD.
YOU'RE A CHIP OFF THE OLD BLOCK, ROD!
DON'T TAKE ANY WOODEN NICKELS, KIDS!
THEY SAY ABSENCE MAKES THE HEART GROW FONDER...BUT PARTING IS SUCH SWEET SORROW!
OH, DEAR.

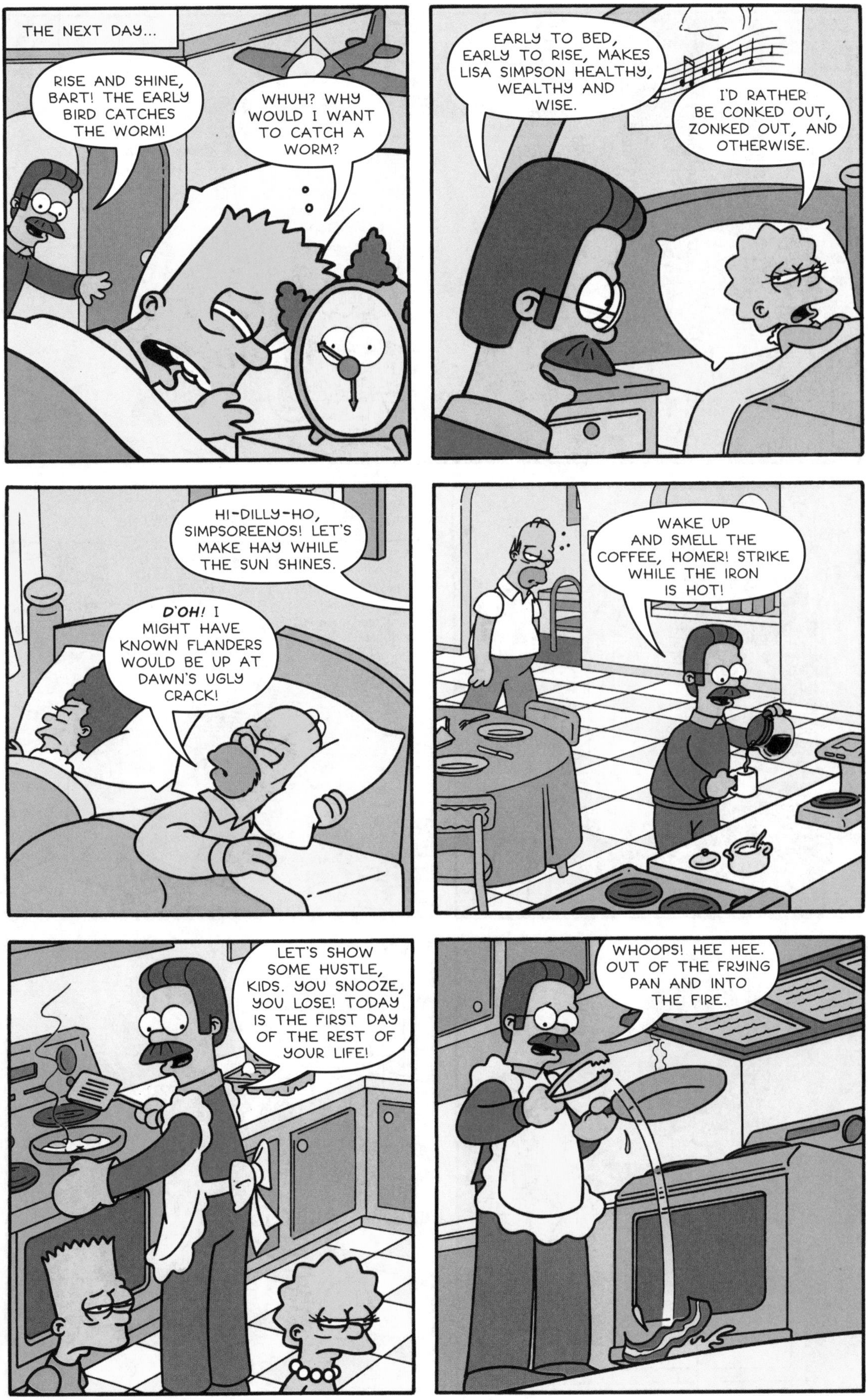

THE NEXT DAY...
RISE AND SHINE, BART! THE EARLY BIRD CATCHES THE WORM!
WHUH? WHY WOULD I WANT TO CATCH A WORM?
EARLY TO BED, EARLY TO RISE, MAKES LISA SIMPSON HEALTHY, WEALTHY AND WISE.
I'D RATHER BE CONKED OUT, ZONKED OUT, AND OTHERWISE.
HI-DILLY-HO, SIMPSOREENOS! LET'S MAKE HAY WHILE THE SUN SHINES.
D'OH! I MIGHT HAVE KNOWN FLANDERS WOULD BE UP AT DAWN'S UGLY CRACK!
WAKE UP AND SMELL THE COFFEE, HOMER! STRIKE WHILE THE IRON IS HOT!
LET'S SHOW SOME HUSTLE, KIDS. YOU SNOOZE, YOU LOSE! TODAY IS THE FIRST DAY OF THE REST OF YOUR LIFE!
WHOOPS! HEE HEE. OUT OF THE FRYING PAN AND INTO THE FIRE.

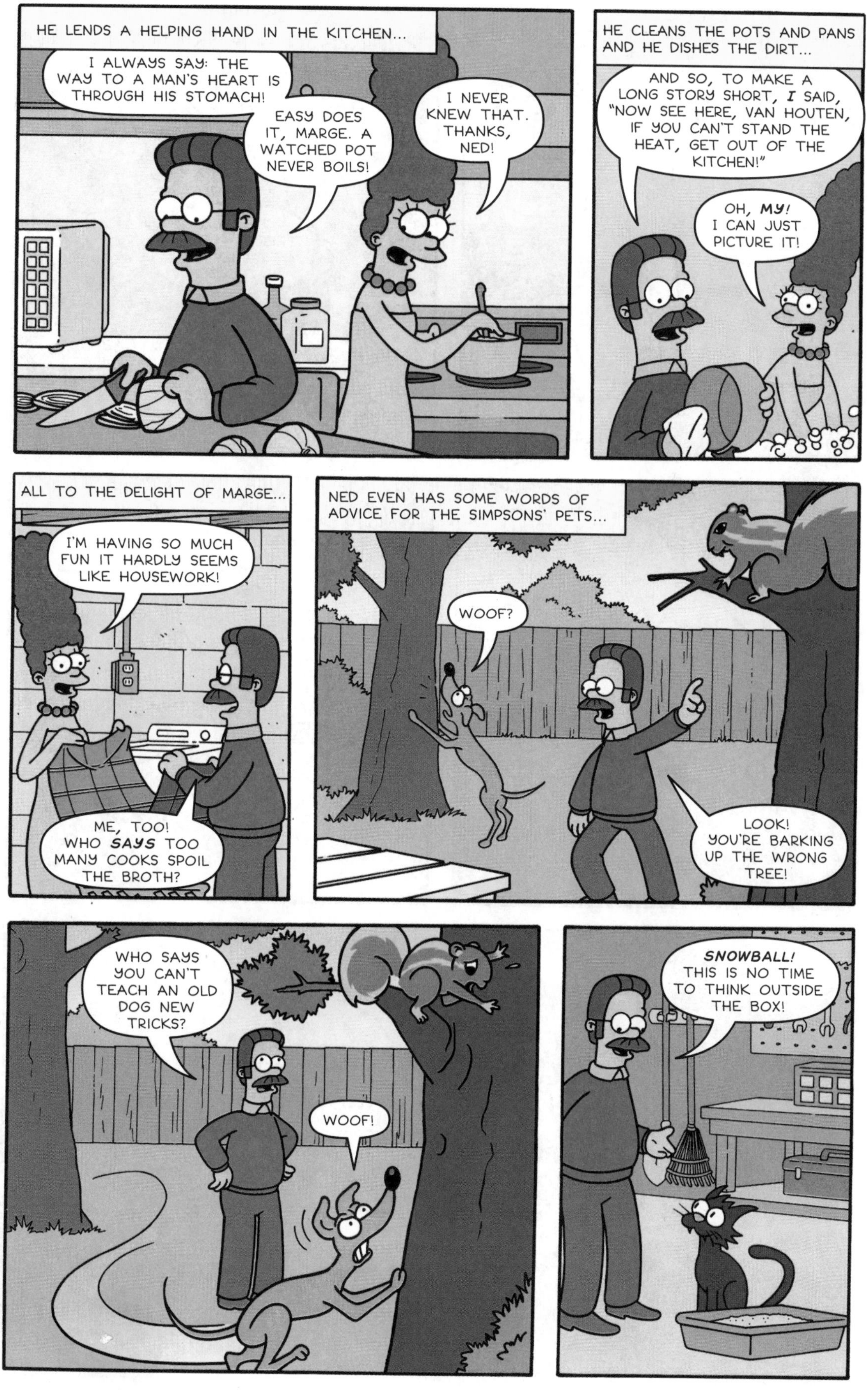
HE LENDS A HELPING HAND IN THE KITCHEN...
I ALWAYS SAY: THE WAY TO A MAN'S HEART IS THROUGH HIS STOMACH!
EASY DOES IT, MARGE. A WATCHED POT NEVER BOILS!
I NEVER KNEW THAT. THANKS, NED!
HE CLEANS THE POTS AND PANS AND HE DISHES THE DIRT...
AND SO, TO MAKE A LONG STORY SHORT, I SAID, "NOW SEE HERE, VAN HOUTEN, IF YOU CAN'T STAND THE HEAT, GET OUT OF THE KITCHEN!"
OH, MY! I CAN JUST PICTURE IT!
ALL TO THE DELIGHT OF MARGE...
I'M HAVING SO MUCH FUN IT HARDLY SEEMS LIKE HOUSEWORK!
ME, TOO! WHO SAYS TOO MANY COOKS SPOIL THE BROTH?
NED EVEN HAS SOME WORDS OF ADVICE FOR THE SIMPSONS' PETS...
WOOF?
LOOK! YOU'RE BARKING UP THE WRONG TREE!
WHO SAYS YOU CAN'T TEACH AN OLD DOG NEW TRICKS?
WOOF!
SNOWBALL! THIS IS NO TIME TO THINK OUTSIDE THE BOX!

LATER...

WHY THE WAIL OF WOE, LISA?

WAAAAAA-AAH!

I HAVE A CRUSH ON THIS CUTE BOY AT THE PARK...AND TODAY I SAW HIM HOLDING HANDS WITH *ANOTHER GIRL!*

OH, WELL. THERE'S PLENTY OF OTHER FISH IN THE SEA.

BUT HE'S BEEN THE LOVE OF MY LIFE FOR *SIX WHOLE DAYS!*

OH, YOU POOR CHILD! I FEEL YOUR PAIN! YOU KNOW, THEY SAY IT IS BETTER TO HAVE LOVED AND LOST THAN NEVER TO HAVE LOVED AT ALL.

AND I ALWAYS SAY: WHEN LIFE GIVES YOU *LEMONS*, MAKE *LEMONADE*. AFTER ALL, LISA, YOU CAN'T WRITE THAT GREAT AMERICAN NOVEL OF YOURS UNTIL YOU'VE EXPERIENCED ALL THE JOY AND SADNESS THAT LIFE HAS TO GIVE.

GEE. YOU'RE *RIGHT!* THANKS, MR. FLANDERS!

ATTA GIRL! NOW LET'S GO DROWN OUR SORROWS IN SOME MILK AND COOKIES.

AND I WON'T CARE HOW THE COOKIES CRUMBLE, AND I WON'T CRY IF THE MILK GETS SPILT. IT'S ALL *GRIST FOR THE MILL!*

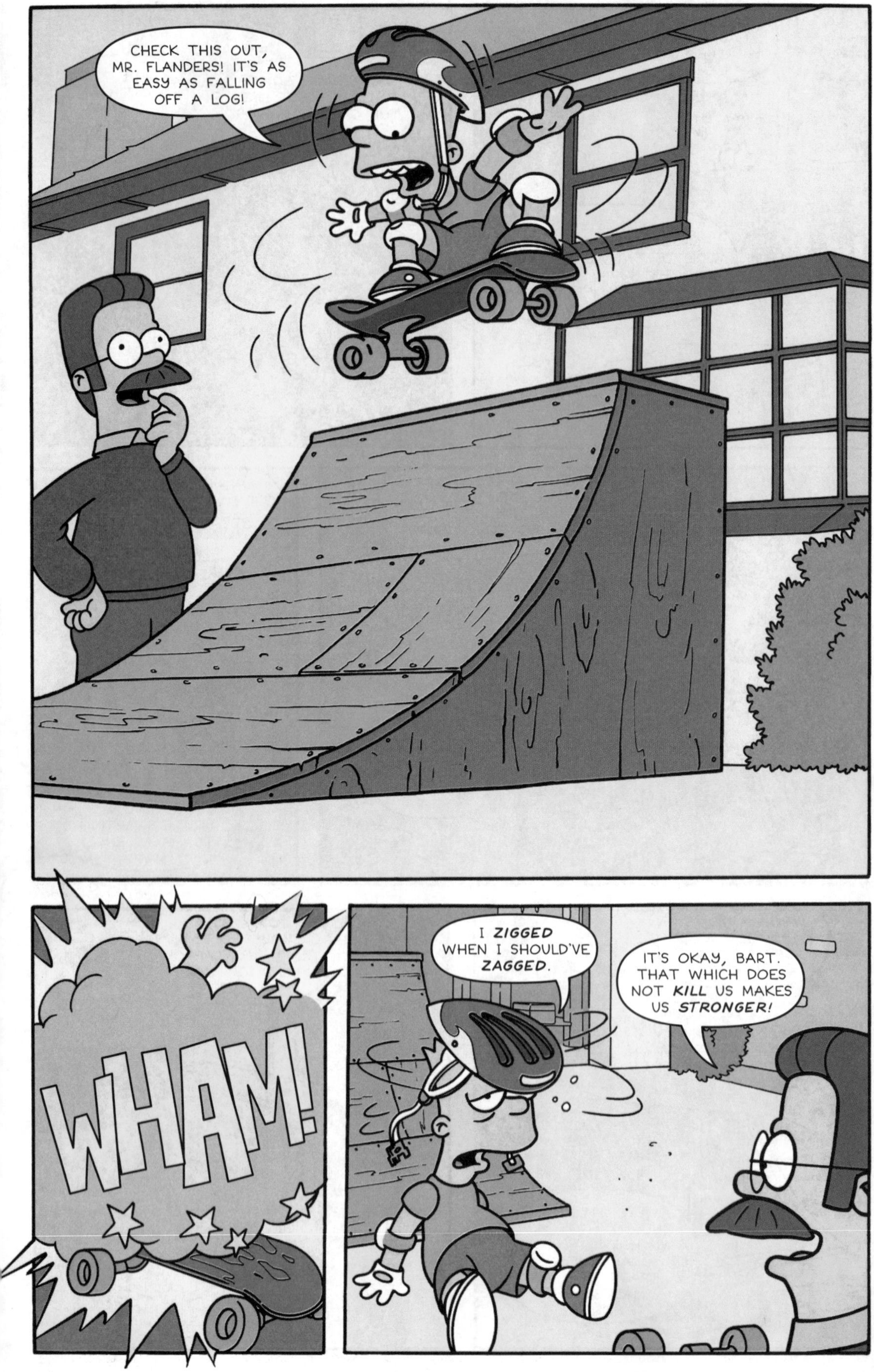
CHECK THIS OUT, MR. FLANDERS! IT'S AS EASY AS FALLING OFF A LOG!
WHAM!
I *ZIGGED* WHEN I SHOULD'VE *ZAGGED*.
IT'S OKAY, BART. THAT WHICH DOES NOT *KILL* US MAKES US *STRONGER*!

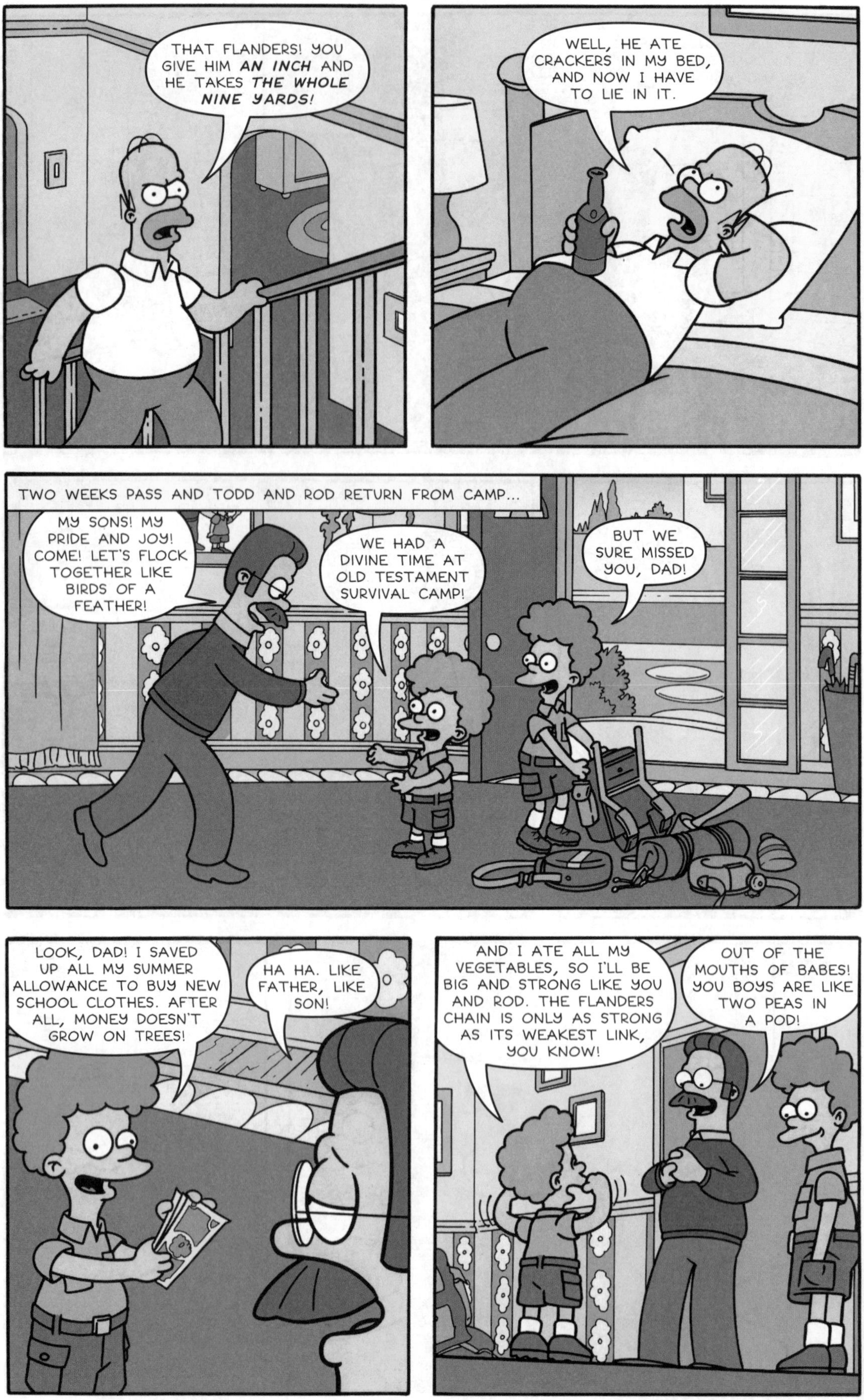
THAT FLANDERS! YOU GIVE HIM **AN INCH** AND HE TAKES **THE WHOLE NINE YARDS!**
WELL, HE ATE CRACKERS IN MY BED, AND NOW I HAVE TO LIE IN IT.
TWO WEEKS PASS AND TODD AND ROD RETURN FROM CAMP...
MY SONS! MY PRIDE AND JOY! COME! LET'S FLOCK TOGETHER LIKE BIRDS OF A FEATHER!
WE HAD A DIVINE TIME AT OLD TESTAMENT SURVIVAL CAMP!
BUT WE SURE MISSED YOU, DAD!
LOOK, DAD! I SAVED UP ALL MY SUMMER ALLOWANCE TO BUY NEW SCHOOL CLOTHES. AFTER ALL, MONEY DOESN'T GROW ON TREES!
HA HA. LIKE FATHER, LIKE SON!
AND I ATE ALL MY VEGETABLES, SO I'LL BE BIG AND STRONG LIKE YOU AND ROD. THE FLANDERS CHAIN IS ONLY AS STRONG AS ITS WEAKEST LINK, YOU KNOW!
OUT OF THE MOUTHS OF BABES! YOU BOYS ARE LIKE TWO PEAS IN A POD!

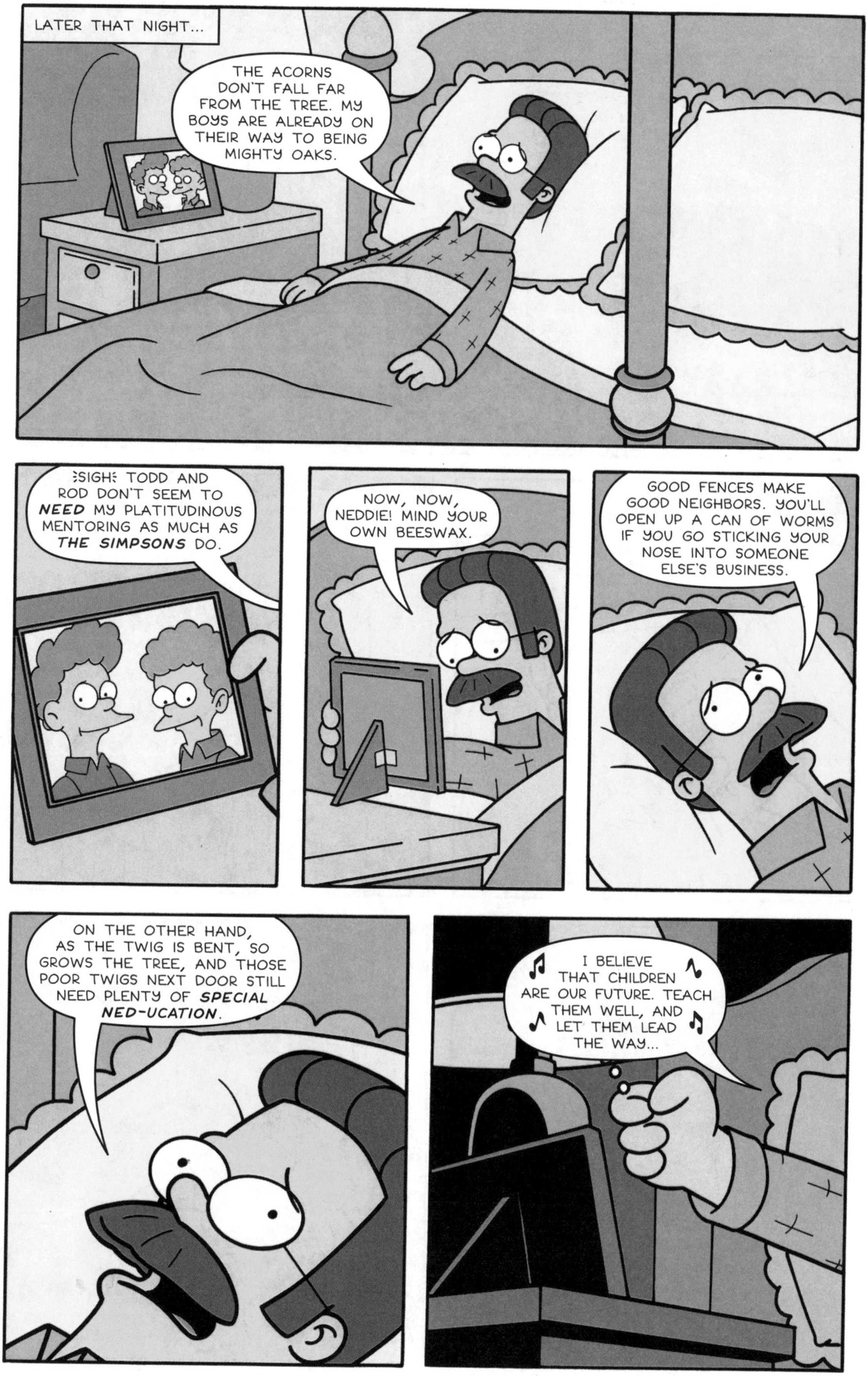
LATER THAT NIGHT...
THE ACORNS DON'T FALL FAR FROM THE TREE. MY BOYS ARE ALREADY ON THEIR WAY TO BEING MIGHTY OAKS.
SIGH TODD AND ROD DON'T SEEM TO NEED MY PLATITUDINOUS MENTORING AS MUCH AS THE SIMPSONS DO.
NOW, NOW, NEDDIE! MIND YOUR OWN BEESWAX.
GOOD FENCES MAKE GOOD NEIGHBORS. YOU'LL OPEN UP A CAN OF WORMS IF YOU GO STICKING YOUR NOSE INTO SOMEONE ELSE'S BUSINESS.
ON THE OTHER HAND, AS THE TWIG IS BENT, SO GROWS THE TREE, AND THOSE POOR TWIGS NEXT DOOR STILL NEED PLENTY OF SPECIAL NED-UCATION.
♪ I BELIEVE THAT CHILDREN ARE OUR FUTURE. TEACH THEM WELL, AND LET THEM LEAD THE WAY... ♪

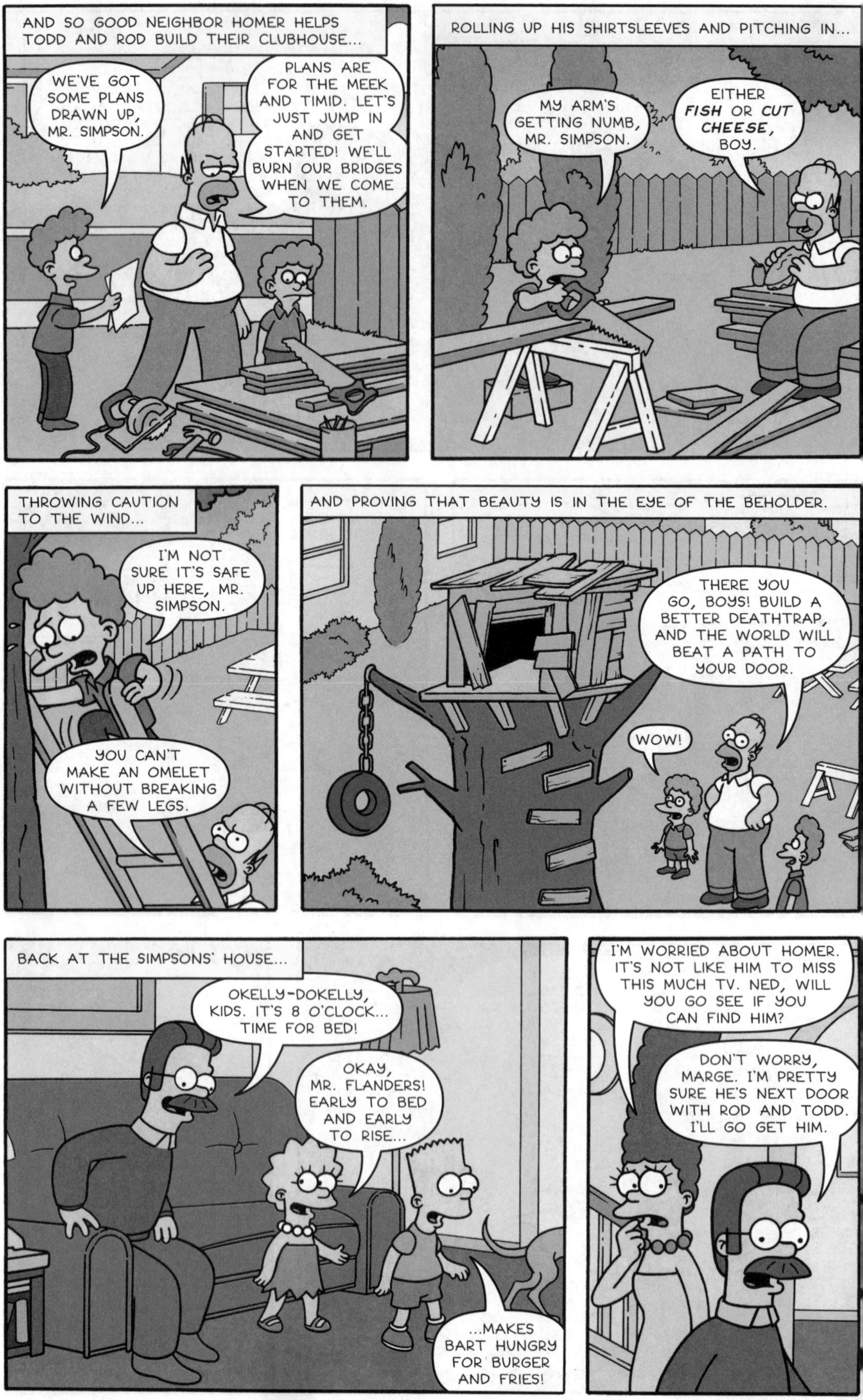
AND SO GOOD NEIGHBOR HOMER HELPS TODD AND ROD BUILD THEIR CLUBHOUSE...
WE'VE GOT SOME PLANS DRAWN UP, MR. SIMPSON.
PLANS ARE FOR THE MEEK AND TIMID. LET'S JUST JUMP IN AND GET STARTED! WE'LL BURN OUR BRIDGES WHEN WE COME TO THEM.
ROLLING UP HIS SHIRTSLEEVES AND PITCHING IN...
MY ARM'S GETTING NUMB, MR. SIMPSON.
EITHER FISH OR CUT CHEESE, BOY.
THROWING CAUTION TO THE WIND...
I'M NOT SURE IT'S SAFE UP HERE, MR. SIMPSON.
YOU CAN'T MAKE AN OMELET WITHOUT BREAKING A FEW LEGS.
AND PROVING THAT BEAUTY IS IN THE EYE OF THE BEHOLDER.
THERE YOU GO, BOYS! BUILD A BETTER DEATHTRAP, AND THE WORLD WILL BEAT A PATH TO YOUR DOOR.
WOW!
BACK AT THE SIMPSONS' HOUSE...
OKELLY-DOKELLY, KIDS. IT'S 8 O'CLOCK... TIME FOR BED!
OKAY, MR. FLANDERS! EARLY TO BED AND EARLY TO RISE...
...MAKES BART HUNGRY FOR BURGER AND FRIES!
I'M WORRIED ABOUT HOMER. IT'S NOT LIKE HIM TO MISS THIS MUCH TV. NED, WILL YOU GO SEE IF YOU CAN FIND HIM?
DON'T WORRY, MARGE. I'M PRETTY SURE HE'S NEXT DOOR WITH ROD AND TODD. I'LL GO GET HIM.

FOR THOSE OF YOU KEEPING SCORE AT HOME, THERE ARE OVER 150 CLICHÉS MENTIONED, MIXED OR MANGLED IN THIS STORY. —EDITOR BILL

THE END

MATT GROENING presents

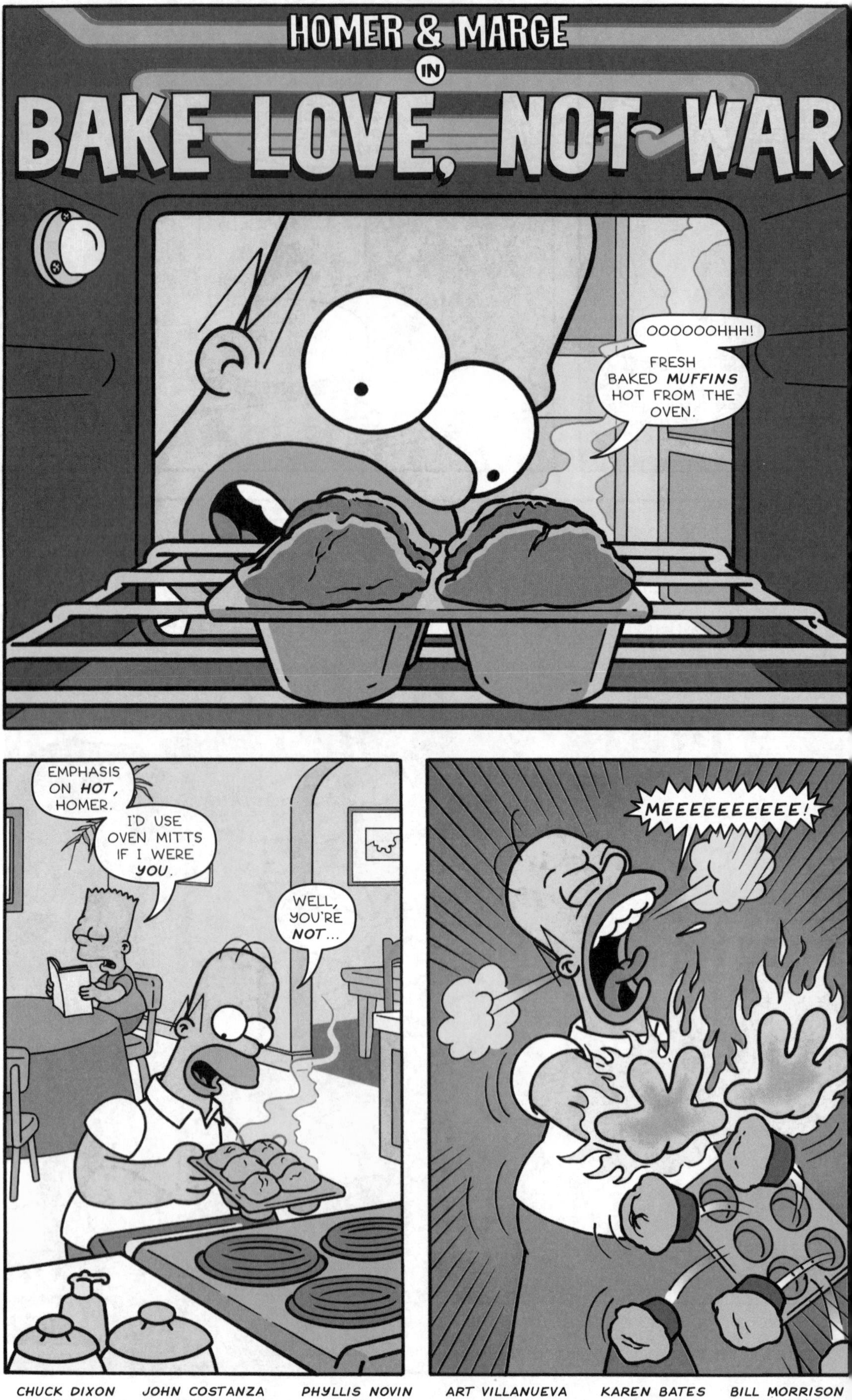
HOMER & MARGE
IN
BAKE LOVE, NOT WAR
OOOOOOHHH!
FRESH BAKED MUFFINS HOT FROM THE OVEN.
EMPHASIS ON HOT, HOMER.
I'D USE OVEN MITTS IF I WERE YOU.
WELL, YOU'RE NOT...
MEEEEEEEEEE!

CHUCK DIXON SCRIPT · JOHN COSTANZA PENCILS · PHYLLIS NOVIN INKS · ART VILLANUEVA COLORS · KAREN BATES LETTERS · BILL MORRISON EDITOR

LEAVE THITH PLATHE, THIMPTHONTH!

HEAD FOR THE CAR, HOMER!

AND TAKE YOUR DEVIL'S FOOD WITH YOU!

THE NEXT DAY...

YOU HUMILIATED ME YESTERDAY IN FRONT OF THE PARENTS AND THE TEACHERS!

I'M RUNNING THE FRIENDSHIP LEAGUE'S PASTA DINNER NIGHT THIS WEEKEND.

AND I NEED YOU TO PROMISE NOT TO COME WITHIN TEN MILES OF THE MEETING HALL!

I PROMISE, MARGE.

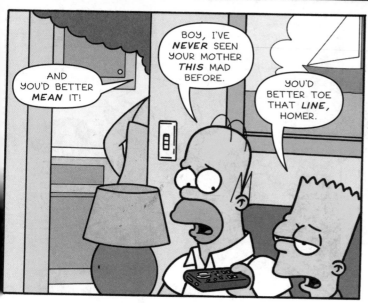

AND YOU'D BETTER MEAN IT!

BOY, I'VE NEVER SEEN YOUR MOTHER THIS MAD BEFORE.

YOU'D BETTER TOE THAT LINE, HOMER.

BUT I HAVE TO WIN BACK HER RESPECT.

YEAH. GOOD LUCK WITH THAT.

I'LL THINK OF SOMETHING THAT CAN'T BACKFIRE!

THAT WEEKEND AT THE MEETING HALL...

SPRINGFIELD FRIENDSHIP LEAGUE PASTA DINNER

WHERE *IS* THAT CATERER I HIRED?

PEOPLE ARE SHOWING UP, AND HE'S NOT *HERE* YET.

SIGNORS AND SIGNORINIS!

NO...

IT'S-A YOUR OLD-A PAISANO, *SPAGHETTI JOE!*

HERE TO SERVE-A YOU SOME-A *HOT AND SPICY MEATBALLS!*

PASTAFAZOOL! HE'S-A AN ETHNIC *STEREOTYPE!*

SOMEBODY SHOULD TAKE THAT LOUSE FOR A *RIDE.*

IT'S PLUMB PO-LITICALLY *ON*CORRECT, I RECKON!

HOMER! HOW *COULD* YOU?

WELL, RENTING THE *MONKEY* WASN'T AS HARD AS I THOUGHT.

BUT I WAS UP ALL *NIGHT* SEWING HIS GONDOLIER OUTFIT.

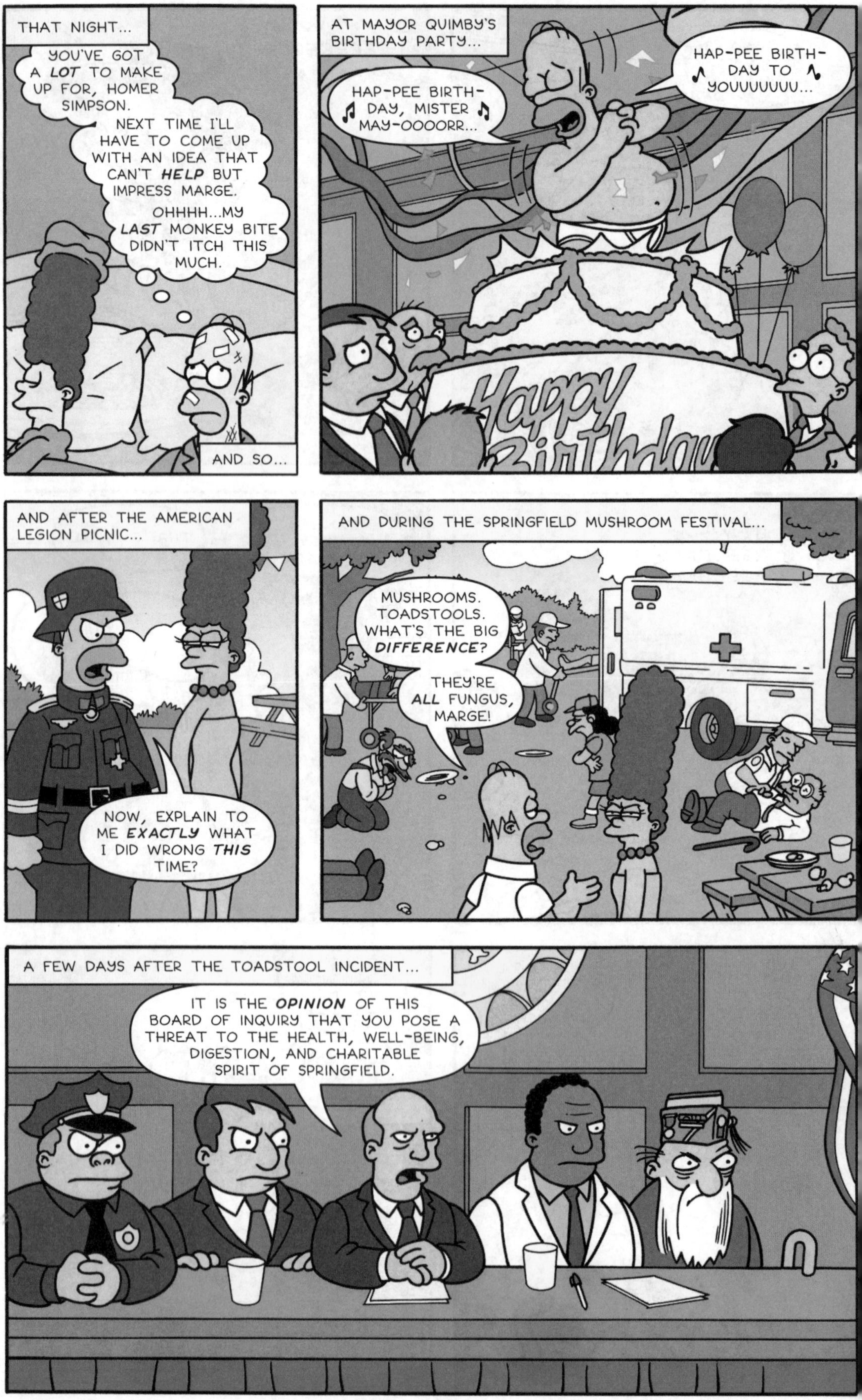
THAT NIGHT...
YOU'VE GOT A LOT TO MAKE UP FOR, HOMER SIMPSON.
NEXT TIME I'LL HAVE TO COME UP WITH AN IDEA THAT CAN'T HELP BUT IMPRESS MARGE.
OHHHH...MY LAST MONKEY BITE DIDN'T ITCH THIS MUCH.
AND SO...
AT MAYOR QUIMBY'S BIRTHDAY PARTY...
HAP-PEE BIRTH-DAY, MISTER MAY-OOOORR...
HAP-PEE BIRTH-DAY TO YOUUUUUUU...
AND AFTER THE AMERICAN LEGION PICNIC...
NOW, EXPLAIN TO ME EXACTLY WHAT I DID WRONG THIS TIME?
AND DURING THE SPRINGFIELD MUSHROOM FESTIVAL...
MUSHROOMS. TOADSTOOLS. WHAT'S THE BIG DIFFERENCE?
THEY'RE ALL FUNGUS, MARGE!
A FEW DAYS AFTER THE TOADSTOOL INCIDENT...
IT IS THE OPINION OF THIS BOARD OF INQUIRY THAT YOU POSE A THREAT TO THE HEALTH, WELL-BEING, DIGESTION, AND CHARITABLE SPIRIT OF SPRINGFIELD.

TONIGHT ON "INSIDE SPRINGFIELD" WE BRING YOU THE LATEST DEVELOP-MENTS ON VICTORIA BURNS VANDERBILT DUPONT BUSH ROCKEFELLER SMYTHE PITT'S UPCOMING MARRIAGE TO GAZILLIONAIRE REGINALD JAMES CABOT WHITNEY III!

FOR THOSE OF YOU KEEPING SCORE AT HOME, THIS MAKES HUSBAND NUMBER SEVEN FOR VICTORIA, THE VIVACIOUS AND STUNNING NIECE OF SPRINGFIELD'S OWN VIVACIOUS AND STUNNING C. MONTGOMERY BURNS...

WILL SOMEONE TURN OFF THAT TV? RIGHT *NOW!!!*

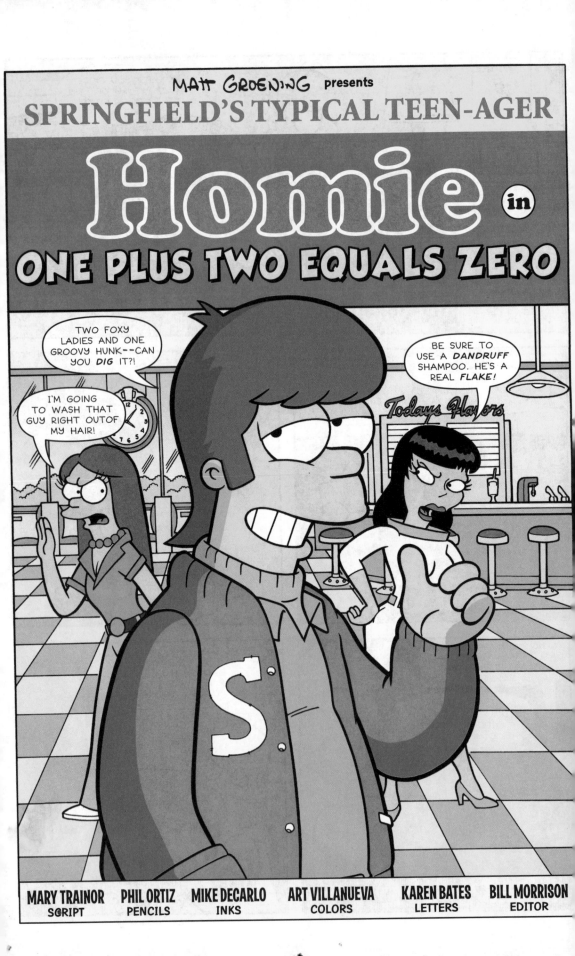

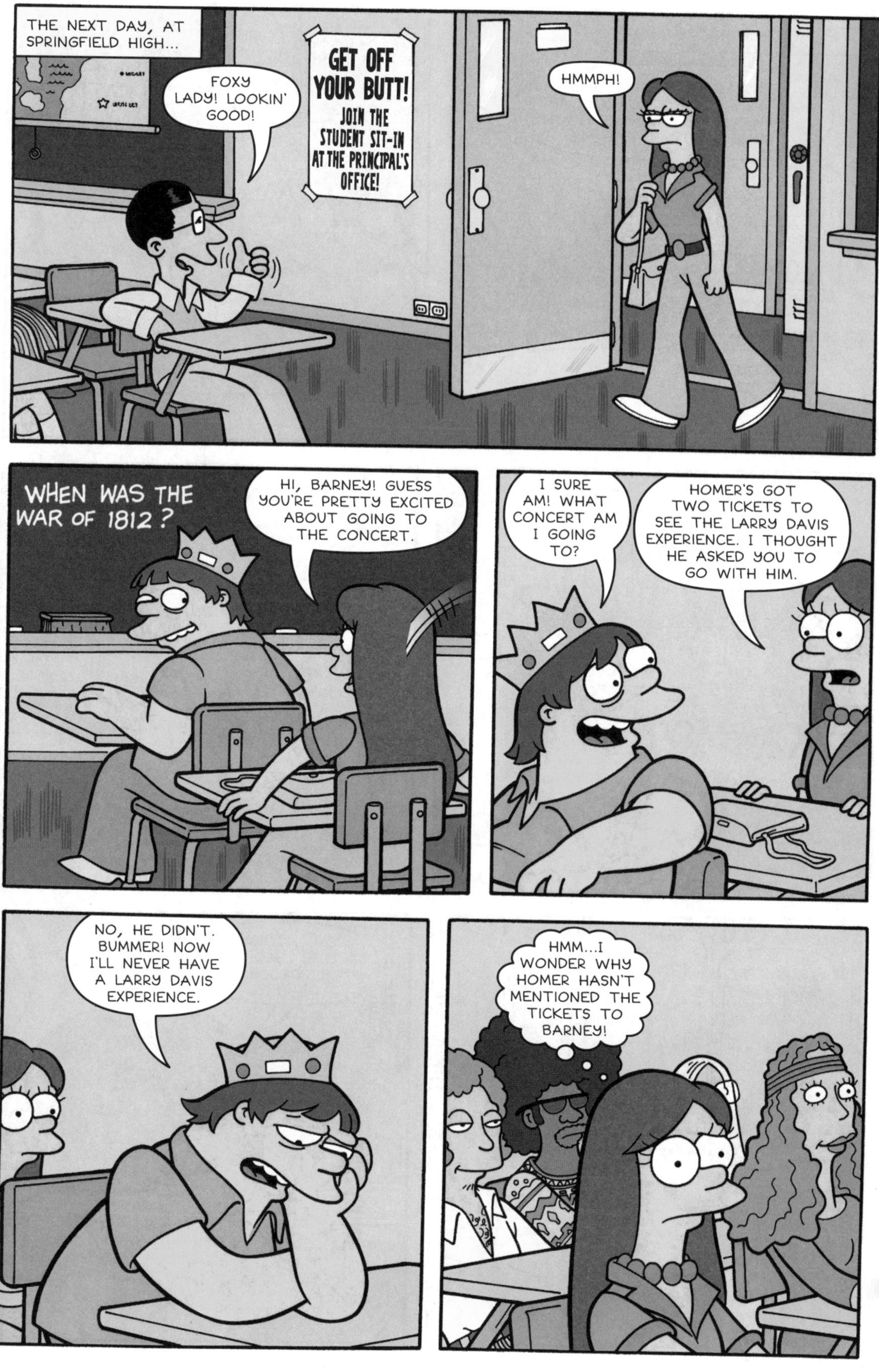
THE NEXT DAY, AT SPRINGFIELD HIGH...
FOXY LADY! LOOKIN' GOOD!
GET OFF YOUR BUTT! JOIN THE STUDENT SIT-IN AT THE PRINCIPAL'S OFFICE!
HMMPH!
WHEN WAS THE WAR OF 1812?
HI, BARNEY! GUESS YOU'RE PRETTY EXCITED ABOUT GOING TO THE CONCERT.
I SURE AM! WHAT CONCERT AM I GOING TO?
HOMER'S GOT TWO TICKETS TO SEE THE LARRY DAVIS EXPERIENCE. I THOUGHT HE ASKED YOU TO GO WITH HIM.
NO, HE DIDN'T. BUMMER! NOW I'LL NEVER HAVE A LARRY DAVIS EXPERIENCE.
HMM...I WONDER WHY HOMER HASN'T MENTIONED THE TICKETS TO BARNEY!

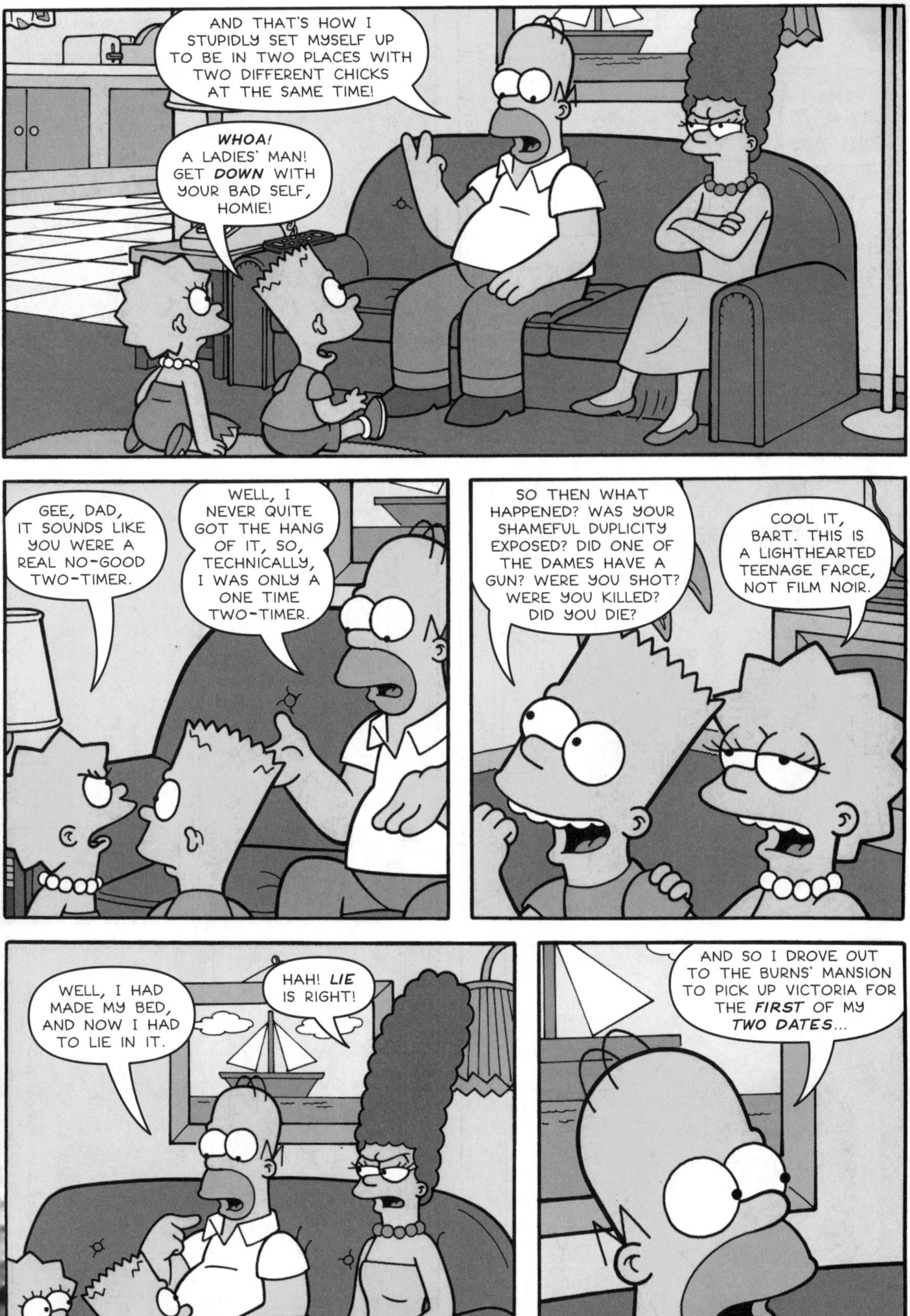
AND THAT'S HOW I STUPIDLY SET MYSELF UP TO BE IN TWO PLACES WITH TWO DIFFERENT CHICKS AT THE SAME TIME!
WHOA! A LADIES' MAN! GET DOWN WITH YOUR BAD SELF, HOMIE!
GEE, DAD, IT SOUNDS LIKE YOU WERE A REAL NO-GOOD TWO-TIMER.
WELL, I NEVER QUITE GOT THE HANG OF IT, SO, TECHNICALLY, I WAS ONLY A ONE TIME TWO-TIMER.
SO THEN WHAT HAPPENED? WAS YOUR SHAMEFUL DUPLICITY EXPOSED? DID ONE OF THE DAMES HAVE A GUN? WERE YOU SHOT? WERE YOU KILLED? DID YOU DIE?
COOL IT, BART. THIS IS A LIGHTHEARTED TEENAGE FARCE, NOT FILM NOIR.
WELL, I HAD MADE MY BED, AND NOW I HAD TO LIE IN IT.
HAH! LIE IS RIGHT!
WOW. MOM SURE DOES HOLD A GRUDGE.
AND SO I DROVE OUT TO THE BURNS' MANSION TO PICK UP VICTORIA FOR THE FIRST OF MY TWO DATES...

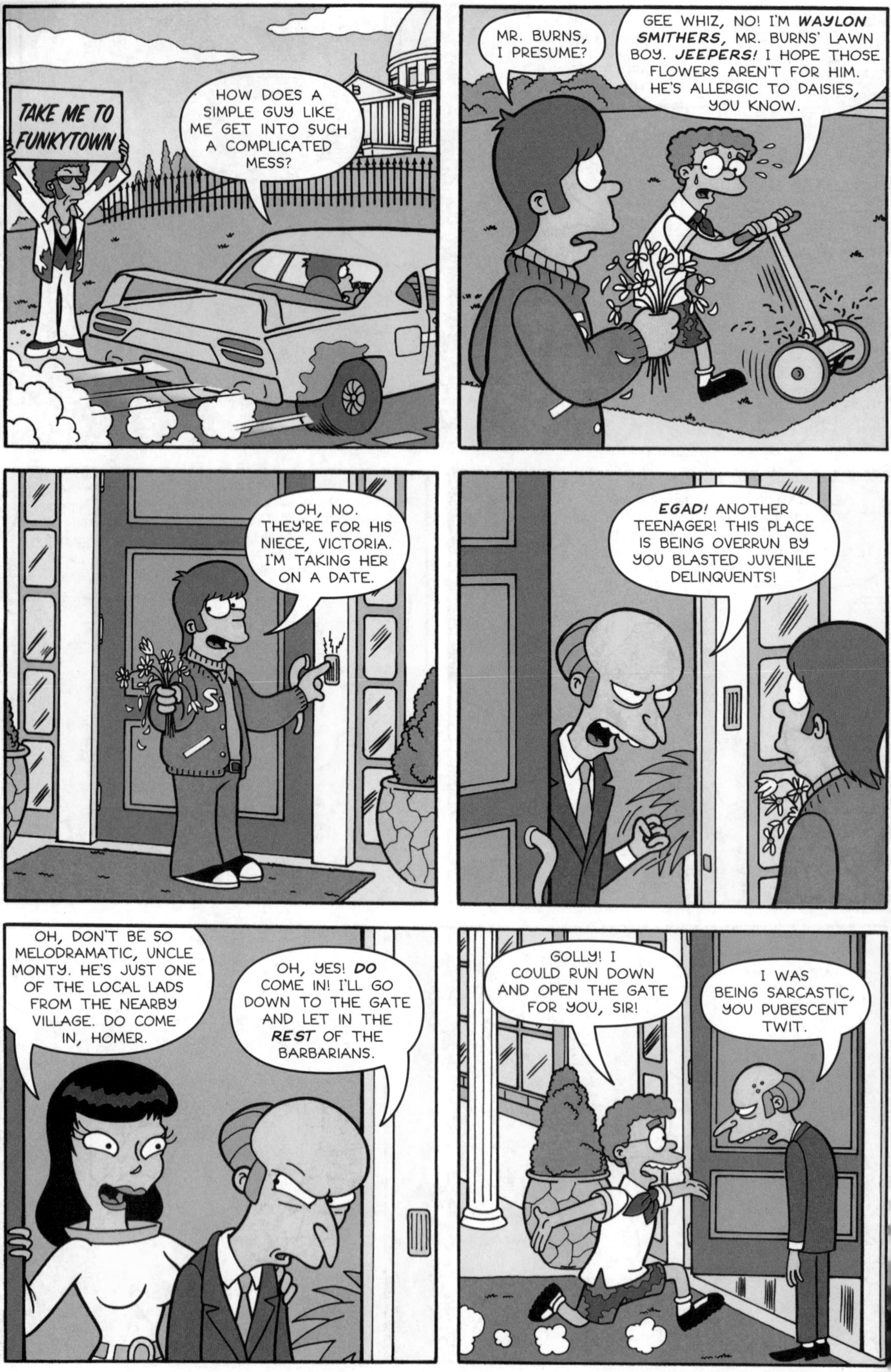
TAKE ME TO FUNKYTOWN
HOW DOES A SIMPLE GUY LIKE ME GET INTO SUCH A COMPLICATED MESS?
MR. BURNS, I PRESUME?
GEE WHIZ, NO! I'M WAYLON SMITHERS, MR. BURNS' LAWN BOY. JEEPERS! I HOPE THOSE FLOWERS AREN'T FOR HIM. HE'S ALLERGIC TO DAISIES, YOU KNOW.
OH, NO. THEY'RE FOR HIS NIECE, VICTORIA. I'M TAKING HER ON A DATE.
EGAD! ANOTHER TEENAGER! THIS PLACE IS BEING OVERRUN BY YOU BLASTED JUVENILE DELINQUENTS!
OH, DON'T BE SO MELODRAMATIC, UNCLE MONTY. HE'S JUST ONE OF THE LOCAL LADS FROM THE NEARBY VILLAGE. DO COME IN, HOMER.
OH, YES! DO COME IN! I'LL GO DOWN TO THE GATE AND LET IN THE REST OF THE BARBARIANS.
GOLLY! I COULD RUN DOWN AND OPEN THE GATE FOR YOU, SIR!
I WAS BEING SARCASTIC, YOU PUBESCENT TWIT.

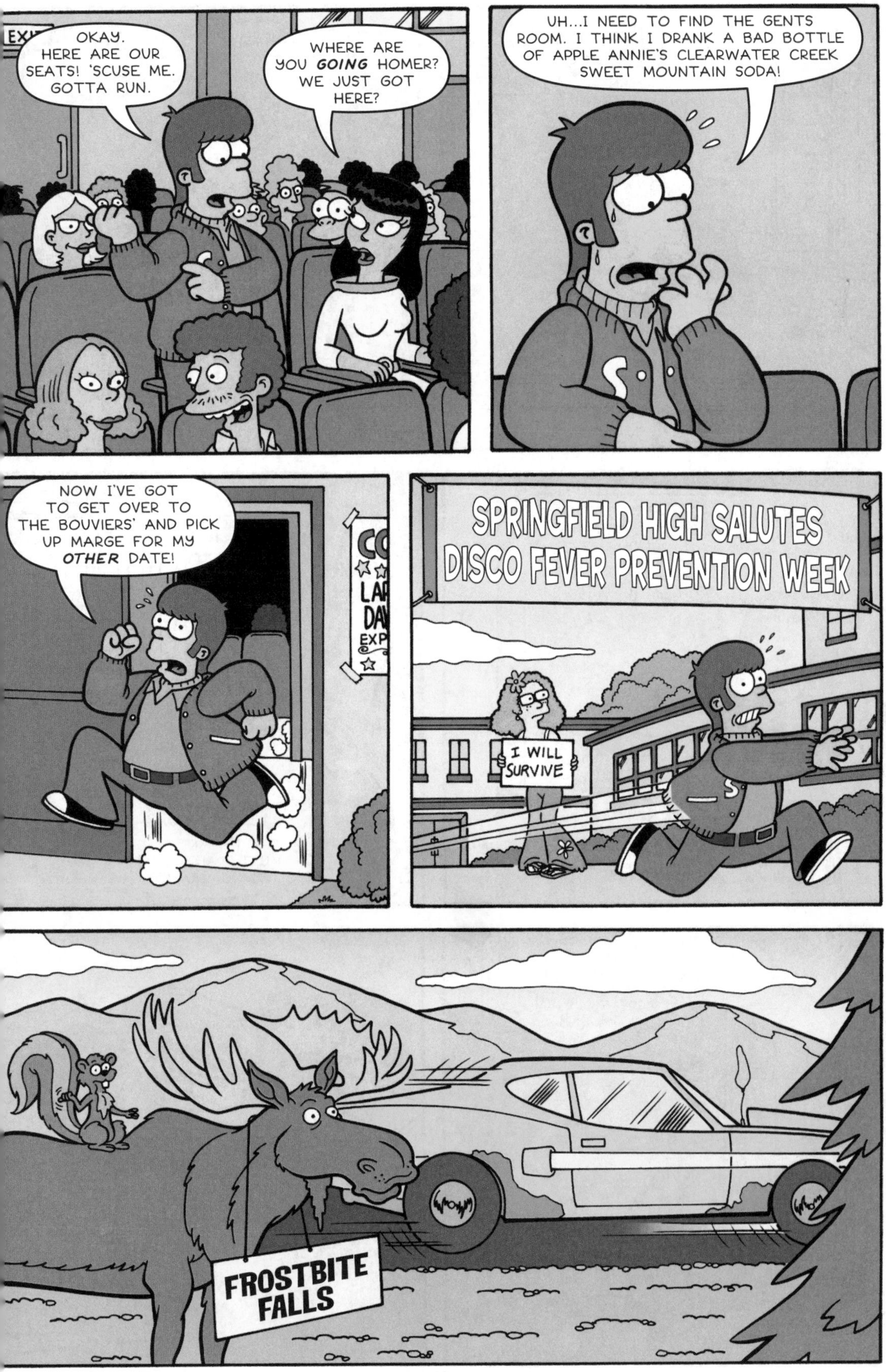
OKAY. HERE ARE OUR SEATS! 'SCUSE ME. GOTTA RUN.
WHERE ARE YOU GOING HOMER? WE JUST GOT HERE?
UH...I NEED TO FIND THE GENTS ROOM. I THINK I DRANK A BAD BOTTLE OF APPLE ANNIE'S CLEARWATER CREEK SWEET MOUNTAIN SODA!
NOW I'VE GOT TO GET OVER TO THE BOUVIERS' AND PICK UP MARGE FOR MY OTHER DATE!
SPRINGFIELD HIGH SALUTES DISCO FEVER PREVENTION WEEK
I WILL SURVIVE
FROSTBITE FALLS

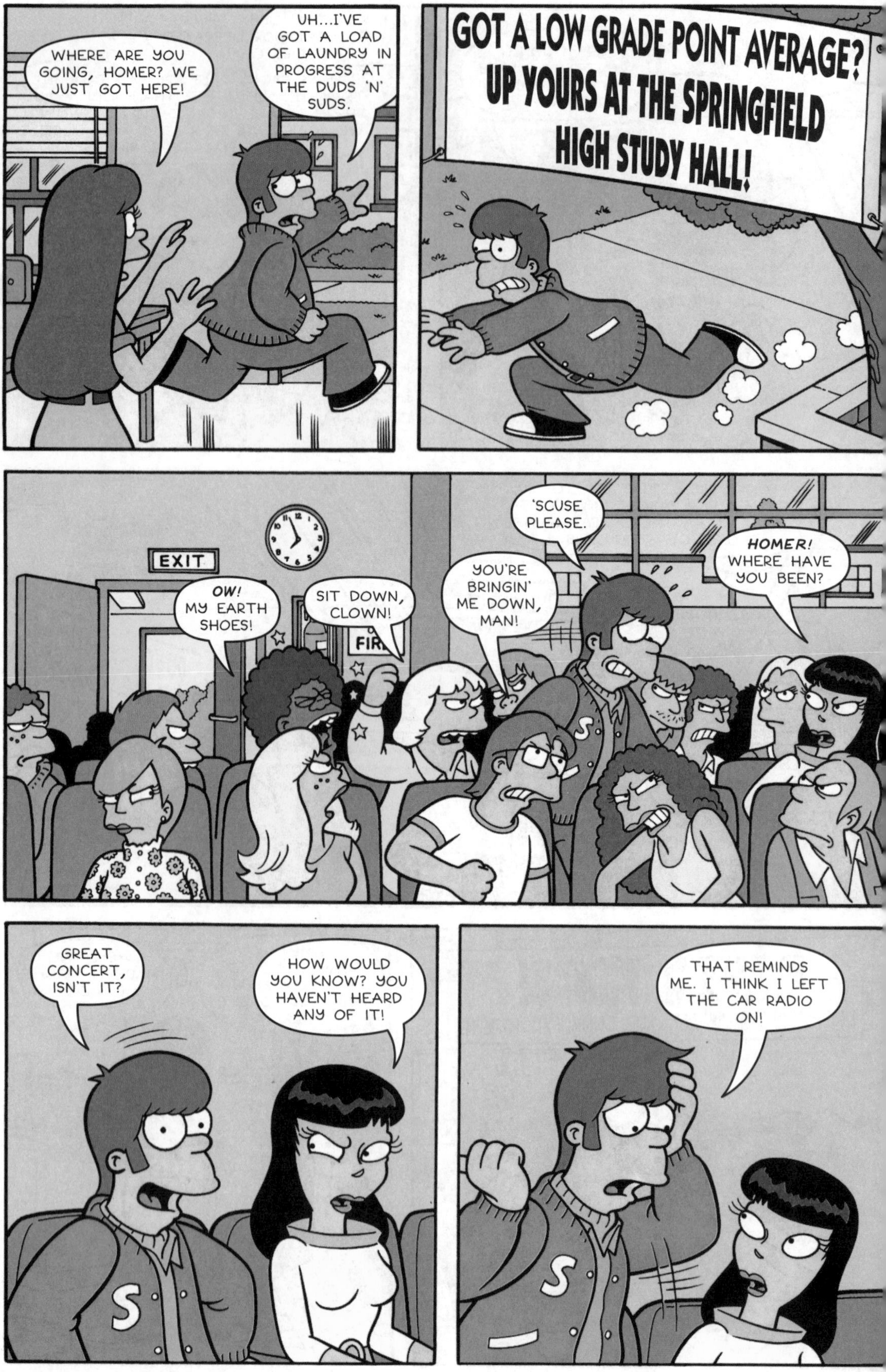
WHERE ARE YOU GOING, HOMER? WE JUST GOT HERE!
UH...I'VE GOT A LOAD OF LAUNDRY IN PROGRESS AT THE DUDS 'N' SUDS.
GOT A LOW GRADE POINT AVERAGE? UP YOURS AT THE SPRINGFIELD HIGH STUDY HALL!
EXIT
OW! MY EARTH SHOES!
SIT DOWN, CLOWN!
YOU'RE BRINGIN' ME DOWN, MAN!
'SCUSE PLEASE.
HOMER! WHERE HAVE YOU BEEN?
GREAT CONCERT, ISN'T IT?
HOW WOULD YOU KNOW? YOU HAVEN'T HEARD ANY OF IT!
THAT REMINDS ME. I THINK I LEFT THE CAR RADIO ON!

SPAZ ALERT!

YOU'RE MESSING UP MY PERM!

HEY! YOU! GET OFF MY CLOUD!

'SCUSE, PLEASE.

HOMER! WHERE DO YOU KEEP RUNNING OFF TO?

EXIT

IN CASE OF FIRE

AND WHERE DID YOU GET THAT BUTTON?

D'OH!

IF I WASN'T SO FILLED TO THE BRIM WITH SELF-ESTEEM, I'D THINK YOU WERE *TWO-TIMING* ME, HOMER!

ME TWO-TIME *YOU*?! HOO BOY! THAT'S FUNNY! IN FACT, IT'S *SO* FUNNY THAT I HAVE TO STEP OUTSIDE AND HAVE A GOOD, HEARTY LAUGH.

I'LL BE RIGHT BACK.

'SCUSE, PLEASE. COMIN' THRU.

I THINK I'LL FOLLOW HIM. STRICTLY AS AN ANTHROPOLOGICAL EXPEDITION, OF COURSE!

THE LIVING END